THE GRAPHIC NOVEL CLASSROOM

For Jack, Shea, Regan, and Riley

"It is the function of art to renew our perception. What we are familiar with we cease to see."

—Anaïs Nin

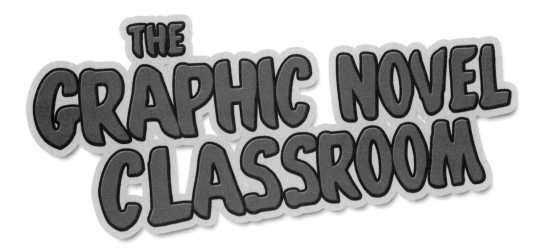

THE GRAPHIC NOVEL CLASSROOM

POWerful

Teaching and Learning With Images

MAUREEN BAKIS

Foreword by
James Bucky Carter

CORWIN
A SAGE Company

372.60445
Bak
1-28-13 1.28

FOR INFORMATION:

Corwin

A SAGE Company

2455 Teller Road

Thousand Oaks, California 91320

(800) 233-9936

Fax: (800) 417-2466

www.corwin.com

SAGE Ltd.

1 Oliver's Yard

55 City Road

London EC1Y 1SP

United Kingdom

SAGE India Pvt. Ltd.

B 1/I 1 Mohan Cooperative Industrial Area

Mathura Road, New Delhi 110 044

India

SAGE Asia-Pacific Pte. Ltd.

33 Pekin Street #02-01

Far East Square

Singapore 048763

Acquisitions Editor: Carol Chambers Collins

Associate Editor: Megan Bedell

Editorial Assistant: Sarah Bartlett

Production Editor: Amy Schroller

Copy Editor: Trey Thoelcke

Typesetter: C&M Digitals (P) Ltd.

Proofreader: Sue Irwin

Indexer: Judy Hunt

Cover Designer: Rose Storey

Permissions Editor: Adele Hutchinson

Copyright © 2012 by Corwin

Printed in the United States of America

Library of Congress Cataloging-in-Publication Data

Bakis, Maureen.
The graphic novel classroom: powerful teaching and learning with images/Maureen Bakis; foreword by James Bucky Carter.

p. cm.
Includes bibliographical references and index.

ISBN 978-1-4129-3684-2 (pbk. : acid-free paper)

1. Comic books, strips, etc., in education. 2. Graphic novels in education. I. Title.

LB1044.9.C59B35 2012
372.6′044—dc23   2011034049

This book is printed on acid-free paper.

11 12 13 14 15 10 9 8 7 6 5 4 3 2 1

Contents

Additional materials and resources related to *The Graphic Novel Classroom* can be found on the companion website.
www.corwin.com/graphicnovelclassroom

List of Classroom Teaching Tools on the Companion Website

Foreword

In 2007, in the introductory chapter to *Building Literacy Connections With Graphic Novels: Page by Page, Panel by Panel*, I wrote that "Although it is hoped that teachers might be convinced by this collection of essays and similar works to try comics or graphic novels in the classroom, more needs to be written to be sufficiently compelling for the most conservative educators" (p. 13). While I do not claim credit for the many comics-and-literacy articles and books that have been published since then, it is nice to see so many teacher-educators, humanities scholars, librarians, graduate students, and practicing teachers adding to the body of research regarding comics and literacy: a corpus, by the way, that stretches at least as far back as the 1940s. Comics and education are linked and have been for decades—centuries even, if we take into account the connections between contemporary graphica and related forms of sequential art. As I tell my students, "Anyone who has sight is a visual learner." Humans are wired to learn visually, and the image-text interface will always be a means of learning, recording, sharing, and knowing. While I know there are still educators reluctant to integrate comics into the curriculum, to embrace fully the utility and history of the image, I take heart in the growing number of educators who see that doing so is no more a "fad" than blue jeans or movies, both of which were coming into the American consciousness around the same time as comic strips.

With so many folks now mining the intersections of graphica and literacy, though, the question of ethos, or expertise and authority, must be addressed. Where does authority reside in contemporary English language arts (ELA) regarding the integration of comics and graphic novels? Within the data sets of the quantitive researcher? Within the case studies of the qualitatively minded professor? Within the well-written essay of a person deemed by fans of the form as an intelligent expert? The librarian? The teacher? The comics art creator?

To me, the question is highly connected to the more general inquiry of where authority resides now in education as a whole. One of my favorite articles of the past few years addressing this question is Frederick M. Hess's "The New Stupid" (2008). Hess suggests that while the current emphasis on quantitative data in education and education studies is appropriate, such data may also be misused or overused. Authority, Hess seems to say, doesn't reside just in the numbers. Qualitative researchers and those employing mixed-methods would be quick to agree. Having been trained as a humanities scholar before becoming an English educator, I tend to see data-driven research as just another rhetorical tradition and approach to understanding, with inherent flaws just like any other. However, I often feel that nowadays the English in ELA is being ignored in favor of senses of ethos that devalue humanities and practitioner-based ways of knowing and communicating. For example, I see shifts in the types of articles some journals are publishing, shifts away from the rich humanities traditions that still have an important place for practicing professionals; in comics-and-literacy related work, specifically, sometimes I notice articles passing peer-review without referencing salient examples of preceding work that should be known and referenced; and I see a variety of campuses remarketing themselves as research-focused at the expense of being seen as teaching-centered. While I understand some of the reasons behind these shifts, I often feel like important nuances are being erased from the discourse of contemporary education and from what it means to be involved in a field like English education that should always bridge the humanities and the social sciences.

To be fair, sometimes I see comics creators making blanket statements about learning without any mention of educational theory or figures. I have seen scholars in other fields and comics advocates make claims about teaching and comics as if simply "saying it makes it so." Because of these things, I am quick to share with my own students, who I do hope will come to see themselves as teacher-researchers, this maxim: all research is important, and all research is bullshit. That is to say, when it comes to education and one's practice thereof, consider everything as if it has something "valid" to offer, but always consider that it might have some flawed and limited theses, and try to figure out what those flaws and limits might be. Nothing, not even write-ups of quantitative data, can give us the complete answer: no one source, no one method, no single expertise.

So, where does authority reside in ELA today? Where does it reside in the intersections of comics and education? The answer is that it must reside in multiple sources. The rusting melting pot of intellectual ideas and pedagogy must morph into a dinner table, where there are many dishes to choose from and room for everyone. That is why I am so pleased with the effort you are about to read. While many comics-and-literacy scholars do have experience using graphica in K–12 settings and have written about those experiences, many of us teach at the university level now. That's not to say we don't ever interact in K–12 schools, but I think we'd all be quick to say that our roles and responsibilities at our universities are not exactly the same as they were when we taught full-time in elementary, middle, or high schools. Maureen's chapters are rooted in current actual practice with contemporary American adolescents. She knows what works and what hasn't and knows how to use real-time teacher research—the hit-or-miss, messy, sometimes instinctual, often "based-in-theory-and-scholarly-research-but-not-a-slave-to-it" kind of information that teachers gather, sort, and analyze every day, on the go, while balancing a hundred other stimuli.

Maureen shares experiences and artifacts from what she calls "the graphic novel classroom," a place where "students liked to read and authentic literacy occurred." She shares nothing she hasn't used or reflected upon, and as you begin to integrate or adjust the ideas in these chapters to your own classrooms, she will be doing the same. You and your students will put your own authentic marks on the texts, strategies, and ideas shared herein, and you will never be alone in creating your own secondary graphic novel classrooms as long as Maureen Bakis is teaching and retooling alongside her kids in Topsfield, Massachusetts.

With great pleasure, I announce Maureen Bakis's place at the table, and I know I can speak for both of us when I say we welcome you to pull up a chair, dig in, and add your own flavor and dishes to the spread. Ultimately, after all, ethos in education or anywhere else doesn't come solely from any one him, her, or them, nor from the producers alone; it comes also from the collective us, the critical consumers who interact with information from multiple sources, look over multiple dishes, if you will, then decide what's best to chew on for a while and what's best to pass.

James Bucky Carter, PhD
Assistant Professor of English Education
University of Texas at El Paso

Preface

Why won't they read? This is the frustrating question I must have asked myself a million times in my first five years as an English teacher. This root problem naturally led to other concerns about literacy—how to teach students basic writing skills, how to get them to think critically, and how get them to problem solve. I spent much of those years trying to reinvent an approach to teaching literature that would cause students to make personal connections to traditional, classic texts in ways that would motivate them to express themselves with passion. I was somewhat successful, but it took an enormous amount of performance from me during class, and honestly, it just felt phony. I was talking too much and leading them too often to make connections that I saw (or thought they *should* see) in lieu of their own authentic responses.

At the same time I was wrestling with this dilemma, I found myself in a graduate class focused entirely on graphic novels. Never a comic book reader myself, I suddenly felt negative and reluctant to read. I was insulted that I was being asked to read something so seemingly irrelevant. What did Batman have to do with me, a forty-year-old single mother? What could I possibly learn from someone like Alan Moore or Scott McCloud? I was angry and skeptical, as I suddenly found myself in the seats of my own students! After I resigned myself to reading these "picture books" to achieve my grade, I found myself falling madly in love. I discovered that Scott McCloud is funny and intriguing and his *Understanding Comics* (1993) blew me away. I wept while reading *Maus* (Spiegelman, 1986) and read *Persepolis* (Satrapi, 2004) three times. *V for Vendetta* (Moore & Lloyd, 1988) resonated with me as I recalled aspects of my undergraduate education as a philosophy major: existentialism, Plato's Allegory of the Cave, and the role of the artist in society. Reading as a teacher, I began to take notes on teachable aspects of all of these incredibly inspiring graphic narratives and wracked my brain about ways I could possibly get these novels into the hands of my students. If I was a reluctant, skeptical reader and I converted, the chances were pretty good students might too. Luckily, just at this time, my high school was considering an English 12 curriculum overhaul, so I jumped at the opportunity to create a course that would focus on graphic novels.

This book is the result of my work to develop a graphic novel classroom, an inviting place at school where students like to read and authentic literacy learning occurs. It is the result of my personal reflections on numerous conversations with students, educators, book distributors, bloggers, librarians, and graphic novelists about teenagers, comics, language arts pedagogy, and twenty-first century learning. When I was searching for information about how to teach graphic novels to high school age students, I looked for resources that exhibited how real students responded to graphic novels and how these texts fostered enjoyment, achievement, and English language arts (ELA) skills. Would teenagers actually read these novels? What would they think if they were being asked to read them in school? I sought answers by investigating how teachers like me were using graphic novels in their classrooms and the degree of success they were experiencing.

A number of outstanding resources authored by educators and professionals informed my development as a graphic novel teacher, including Dr. James Carter's *Building Literacy Connections With Graphic Novels* (2007), which paved the way for teachers like me to publicize their experiences teaching comics. His award-winning book is an edited collection of various educators' ideas for pairing graphic novels with classic texts and contemporary young adult literature. Katie Monnin's *Teaching Graphic Novels: Practical Strategies for the Secondary ELA Classroom* (2010) is another great resource loaded with extensive reading lists, classroom activity templates, and an outstanding cross-index of middle and high school graphic novels and themes. Dr. Michael Bitz's *When Commas Meet Kryptonite* (2010) is yet another excellent book that includes instructional ideas for the classroom based on Dr. Bitz's very successful "Comic Book Project" (Bitz, 2004). These scholars, and other talented professionals in the field, have created useful resources for teaching comics and graphic novels to a range of age groups and academic levels, but this book you are currently reading is the resource I was looking for—comprehensive, text-specific with models of teaching and student learning authored by a high school English teacher for fellow teachers. The text-specific nature of this book, its scope, the unique combination of resources, and its demonstrations of twenty-first century learning, along with student commentary and composition, differentiate it from the current resources available. By default, this book is a solid rationale for including graphic novels in any standard ELA curriculum and adds to the ongoing conversation about comics in education.

In our graphic novel classroom at Masconomet Regional High School, I have students coming after class to ask for the next book in the unit because they have already read ahead through the currently assigned text.

Students are blogging about the best book they've ever read or the first or only book they've ever enjoyed reading in high school. Some of these comments are sprinkled throughout this book. Because of graphic novels and a pedagogy based on transactional theory and reader response, I am finally teaching language arts and twenty-first century skills with students who are as engaged and passionate about what they are reading, writing, and creating in multiple media formats as I am. Our classroom is a happy, creative, and productive place where literacy, including visual literacy, is the norm. I hope you find this book useful in creating the classroom you desire, one that includes graphic novels and the one your students deserve.

Acknowledgments

Thank you, students in the Masconomet Regional High School classes of 2010 and 2011 for your honesty about reading and reading graphic novels. My thanks also go to the English Department chairperson, David Donavel, and our principal, Pam Culver, at Masconomet. If David and Pam hadn't said yes to my idea about comics in the classroom, this book wouldn't exist. I'd also like to thank the Masconomet Regional School Committee for being open-minded and receptive of change, something that happens too infrequently and slowly in education. The School Committee members, many of them parents, saw the need for student choice and more pleasurable reading opportunities in the classroom and made our twelfth grade elective curriculum a reality. Thank you colleagues and friends at Masconomet, first and foremost my mentor teacher, Deborah Shapiro, who helped me navigate the classroom as a new teacher, provided a model of professional excellence, and became my closest friend. My lunch buddies in House C, fellow English department cohorts, especially Alison Prindiville and Annie Rollins, and my special student helper, Victoria Caruso, and Special Education tutor, Cheryl Elkins, also deserve thanks. Christian Leblanc, Chris Love, and Keith Hartan with whom I shared many conversations about comics and graphic novels, thank you!

A special thank you goes to John Shableski, who invited me into the inner circle of graphic novelists, publishers, and researchers, including Dr. James Bucky Carter and Dr. Katie Monnin. Thanks to Cary Gillenwater for sharing his dissertation research about using graphic novels in the classroom and answering my many questions. Our work together combines theory and practice about the power of using comics in classroom to foster student learning and a love of reading.

Any teacher worth her salt realizes that she is only as good as her mentors. In this respect, I credit my parents first for my work ethic and constantly reinforcing the importance and value of education. Professors in the graduate education department at Salem State University all deserve many thanks, including Dr. Lisa Mulman, who introduced me to graphic novels and celebrated my successful use of them in the classroom, Dr. J. D. Scrimgeour, who introduced to me to graphic novel memoir, imagery created by words within poetry, and Dr. Ann Taylor, who taught me how to teach writing. Dr. Donnalee Rubin introduced me to the work of Louise Rosenblatt, Sheridan Blau, Kelly Gallagher, and Jim Burke, whose work informs my classroom practice and is evident throughout this book. I can't thank her enough for teaching me about reading and for the resources she has provided for this book.

Thanks to my siblings, including my sister and very best friend, Arlene Barbieri, Sharon Thurston, Kelly Lacrosse, and my brother, John Bakis, who groomed me to be persistent, moral, mentally tough, and humorous, respectively. Being the youngest certainly has its benefits. And to Rob Hayes, thank you for taking me away from the daily toil to tropical places, providing sanity when I needed it most, and for your patience and love. Last, but certainly not least, my love, my world, and the reason I exist—my children Jack, Shea, Regan, and Riley Doyle—thank you. You have no idea how grateful I am that you willingly share your mom with so many other kids every day and for waiting so patiently for me to finish writing this book. I love you!

Publisher's Acknowledgments

Corwin gratefully acknowledges the contributions of the following reviewers:

Melody Aldrich, English Teacher and Department Chair
Poston Butte High School, Florence, AZ

Kristie Betts Letter, National Board Professional Teacher of Secondary English
Peak to Peak High School, Lafayette, CO

Stergios Botzakis, Assistant Professor, Adolescent Literacy
University of Tennessee, Knoxville, TN

David Callaway, Seventh Grade Social Studies Teacher
Rocky Heights Middle School, Highlands Ranch, CO

Emmalee Callaway, 2nd–3rd Grade Gifted and Talented Teacher
Acres Green Elementary School, Littleton, CO

James Bucky Carter, Assistant Professor of English Education
University of Texas at El Paso

Darlene Castelli, Literacy Coach and Reading Specialist
Clayton High School, Clayton, MO

Douglas Fisher, Professor
School of Teacher Education, San Diego State University, CA

Rachel Hanson, Writing Coach and Eighth Grade Gifted Language
    Arts Teacher
Lakeside Middle School, Forsyth County Schools, Cumming, GA

Lorenza Lara, Secondary Literacy Coordinator
Denver Public Schools, Denver, CO

Linda Parsons, Assistant Professor of Literacy
The Ohio State University

Rebecca Rupert, English Teacher
Bloomington New Tech High School, Monroe County Community
    School Corporation, Bloomington, IN

Anna Soter, Professor, Adult and Adolescent Literacies/English Education
School of Teaching and Learning, The Ohio State University

Cindy A. Spoon, Basic Reading
Montgomery Blair High School, Silver Spring, MD

About the Author

Maureen Bakis is a mother of four children and has been teaching English at Masconomet Regional High School in Topsfield, Massachusetts, for seven years. Maureen presents her experiences teaching graphic novels to high school students at local, regional, and national conferences and events, most recently New York Comic Con, Harvard University's Center for Middle Eastern Studies, and New England Comic Arts in the Classroom. She also blogs about her experiences as webmaster at www.graphicnovelsandhighschoolenglish.com.

Introduction

Welcome to the Graphic Novel Classroom

When students arrive at the graphic novel classroom on the first day of school, they are disoriented because I turn off the lights, project a fifteen-minute TED Talk video (www.ted.com) onto our interactive whiteboard, and sit at a desk along with them to watch. They are expecting me to take attendance and hand out the usual list of materials for English class, but instead, I welcome them with an experience. Together, we look and listen to J. P. Toomey (2010), creator of the daily comic strip, *Sherman's Lagoon*, who discusses his love of cartooning, the ocean, and his desire to protect it through the art of story. After viewing, students discuss their reactions about how Toomey's work for Mission Blue demonstrates the power and importance of storytelling in the comics medium. They get it, immediately. I know what they are thinking: the first day is supposed to be easy, a blow-off, and what is this lady doing? Critical thinking? Viewing? Discussion? Comics as *serious*? This is not what they expected, and I can see doubt about their course selection when they shift in their seats and look at me like I am crazy. They heard this class was easy. They thought it sounded like an easy A. It's not.

After evaluating the story Toomey tells, I ask students to talk to me about the kinds of stories *they* tell and why and how they tell them. I also poll them about their reading experiences in and outside of school. Don't tell me what you think I want to hear, I say—that will be our mantra for the year, and I have to communicate it early and often. I ask them to be honest and they are. Some say they hate reading. Others say they like to read but hate school reading. Teachers ruin books, they say, by overanalyzing them and making students overanalyze them. They took this course because it sounded easy and fun. It sounded different and they want different. And so we begin our adventure together in the graphic novel classroom.

WARNING: READING COMICS IS NOT SO EASY

One of the very next things I do is address the common and incorrect assumption that reading and understanding graphic novels is simple. Teaching graphic novels to students has taught me that it is important to avoid the assumption that *all* students are familiar with reading comics merely because comics are most often associated with kids. Because of the common stereotypes surrounding comics as childish or outlandish, students sometimes feel worse for knowing little about the medium. It is therefore important to establish a baseline of students' initial understanding of comics and their level of exposure to graphic novels before studying specific texts. The last thing you want your students to feel reading these challenging and complex texts is stupid. Most of them have had enough of that already. I ask my students to answer a few basic questions that stress their personal experience and interpretation because I want them to realize right away that what they say matters and their interpretations are valued. This is the beginning of teaching students through the use graphic novels how to find their own voice.

WHY GRAPHIC NOVELS?

There are several good reasons to use graphic novels in your classroom. My reasons are based on classroom practice, observations, and conversations with students, some of which have been confirmed by other educators:

- Students read graphic novels. They don't pretend to read.
- Because I can teach more graphic novel titles in the same amount of time I'd spend teaching fewer lengthier print texts, students are privy to a wide variety of stories and genres that keep them continually engaged in reading.
- Graphic novels and other shorter graphic narratives can be read in the classroom, thus I can facilitate students' application of reading strategies and clarify trouble spots for students for an enjoyable read. Students love the time I give them without distractions at home. This builds sustained attention for reading and students are less likely to quit reading a challenging text. Plus, it's social. When everyone around you is reading, it's hard not to follow the crowd. Many students find this "relaxing" and "look forward to reading in English." Those are students' words, not mine.
- Because they take less time to read, graphic novels are easier to reread for deeper comprehension, so students are more apt to experience reading as a constructive, recursive process (Diamond Bookshelf, 2008).

- Reading graphic novels adds to students' reading repertoire (and my teaching repertoire).
- Students find the aesthetic experience with visuals pleasurable (as opposed to more typical anesthetic experiences associated with common types of school-based reading).
- Because of the interpretive nature of pictures, graphic novels facilitate instruction on the participatory and active, constructive nature of reading (Diamond Bookshelf, 2008; Gillenwater, 2009).
- Because images are open for interpretation, this prompts rich discussion, stimulates problem solving, and builds social meaning (Gillenwater, 2010); therefore, students avoid one authoritative answer, creating a more democratic classroom (Rosenblatt, 1995).
- With graphic novels, students can learn how to handle ambiguity in a text, develop an open-minded approach to its possibilities, sustain attention, and develop other traits of competent readers (Blau, 2003).
- Students build confidence reading graphic novels, promoting further engagement with other forms of storytelling and chang[ing] negative attitudes toward reading (Panella, 2004).
- Students feel respected for getting to read books they like, in school.
- The content within graphic novels lends itself to exploration of big picture or essential questions, fostering students' personal and intellectual growth.
- The analysis of the relationship between content and form of graphic novels prompts critical thinking and is applicable to analysis of other media (Diamond Bookshelf, 2008).
- Graphic novels challenge weak and strong readers alike.
- Students must exercise more skill (reading images and text) not fewer when reading graphic novels (Gillenwater, 2010; Yannicopoulou as cited in McPherson, 2006).
- The comics medium and themes found in graphic novels are more connected to students' experiences and more personally relevant to their lives. They don't often get bored reading and give up.
- Because students are more invested and engaged in graphic novels, their writing is more interesting, authentic, and passionate. This provides more opportunity to facilitate writing instruction and skill development.
- Quotable images are easier to recall and locate in text to cite when providing evidence to support analysis and interpretation.
- Critical analyses and prefabricated essays about graphic novels are not yet ubiquitous on the Internet; therefore, critical thinking, analysis, and writing must come from students rather than from a field of "experts" from whom they might "borrow" interpretations, a common problem when teaching traditional texts or classic works of fiction.

- They are useful in meeting curriculum standards and twenty-first century skills (Partnership for 21st Century Skills, 2009).
- They are fun to teach!

PEDAGOGICAL INFLUENCES

In addition to choosing engaging material, pedagogy is the other important factor in getting and keeping kids reading in school. Teachers can potentially spoil the experience of reading great stories if they try to control how students respond to them. As is evident throughout this book, my pedagogy is informed by Louise Rosenblatt's transactional theory and a reader response approach to teaching literature.

Transactional Theory

When I use the term *transactional theory*, I am referring to Louise Rosenblatt's explanation of the reading process in *Literature as Exploration* (1995) as transaction between a reader and a literary text. The reading process is "a constructive, selective process over time in a particular context" wherein "[t]he relation between reader and signs on the page proceeds in a to-and-fro spiral, in which each is continually being affected by what the other has contributed" (p. 26).

Reader Response

When I refer to my pedagogical approach as based on *reader response*, I mean that my role as teacher is to design lessons and a classroom environment that presupposes that my students' experience with a text is transactional as Rosenblatt (1995) defines it. Readers' personal, distinct responses are of primary importance in contrast to a teacher imposing his or her interpretation of a text or leading students to understand a text in one, correct, authoritative, or predetermined way.

Practical classroom methodologies, lesson activities, and assessments throughout this book are also influenced by the approach to literacy outlined in Sheridan Blau's *The Literature Workshop* (2003). Especially apparent in Chapters 2 and 6 are his influence on reading and writing as a recursive process, and his "marks of competent readers" (p. 210) are habits I aim to help my students practice while reading graphic novels. The seven traits include: capacity for sustained, focused attention; willingness to suspend closure; willingness to take risks, tolerance for failure; tolerance for ambiguity, paradox, and uncertainty; intellectual generosity; and fallibilism and metacognitive awareness (p. 211). In addition to Rosenblatt and Blau, the Partnership for 21st Century Skills (2009), Kelly Gallagher (2004, 2009), and Jim Burke (1999, 2000, 2010) also influence my methods.

Twenty-First Century Skills

When I refer to twenty-first century skills or twenty-first century learning in this book, I am referring to the learning and innovation skills that include creativity and innovation, critical thinking and problem solving, and communication and collaboration, as well as the information, media, and technology skills outlined in the Partnership for 21st Century Skills Framework Definitions (2009).

Additional resources regarding theory, methodology, and reading graphic novels are listed in the References of this book.

A WORD ABOUT ASSESSMENT

Since I subscribe to teaching that fosters student-centered, constructive learning, my primary goal in this book is to show you the *process* of learning with graphic novels. I want to show you the trial and error, epiphanies, and musings and reflections of students who are reading graphic novels and constructing comics of their own. Philosophically, I believe teachers should collaborate with students to create appropriate rubrics that target specifically tailored goals for their particular population and use assessment data to continually adjust future lesson activities and plan curriculum. This very fluid process is difficult to capture by way of generic scoring guides.

My students and I co-construct rubrics, which take into consideration students' individual composition goals, and we conference often to adjust expectations, depending on the direction the composition piece takes. We discuss and attempt to visualize final products and the specific aspects assignments will include, though we are careful to allow for creativity and innovation during the composition process, otherwise students are somewhat prohibited from taking risks and using composition as discovery. It takes more time and more energy from both teacher and student to be invested in constructing differentiated rubrics, and the easy way out is to default to a less democratic approach, but I urge you and your students to determine together what an "A" looks like for the particular exercises in literacy learning you find throughout this book. The other reason specific scoring guides are absent from the chapters is simply because I use a quarterly portfolio assessment system based on Sheridan Blau's method outlined in *The Literature Workshop* (2003), wherein most grading takes place on biquarterly and quarterly bases; however, sample assessments are available at the companion website (www.corwin.com/graphicnovelclassroom) that you might adjust to fit your students' needs.

LET THEM DRAW PICTURES

You will notice throughout this book that my approach to teaching graphic novels emphasizes both reading images and composing with them. When I first began teaching graphic novels, I was cautious about allowing students to draw pictures in English class because I thought it might interfere with teaching writing. I soon realized that in order for students to truly understand and appreciate comics as a storytelling and communications medium that I had to let them try their hand at composing sequential art. Students were concerned that they would be graded on their drawing skills, but I reassured them (as many graphic artists do at comics workshops) that stick-figures are perfectly acceptable, and I drew alongside them for reassurance. Once students realize they are allowed to play, they quickly enter into creative mode!

Since the world today is full of multimedia and professional presentations that typically contain visual elements, it simply makes sense to prepare students to work with images as part of their developing language skill. The various student artwork in the book and their comics research presentations posted online reveal practice using visuals to entertain, tell story, and convey information almost always for a real audience. At first, my students were afraid to draw, but I allowed them a wide range of tools to accomplish the task of creating visual narratives and many took advantage of learning new technologies, whereas others preferred to use the low-tech pencil-and-paper approach. If you plan to teach graphic novels and ask your students to draw, I recommend looking on the companion website for links to resources for illustrating and creating comics.

CHAPTER SNAPSHOTS

This book is meant to help you see the kinds of teaching and learning that occurs in a graphic novel classroom. I think of the chapters as a collection of snapshots of graphic novel lessons, activities, student discussion, and composition using specific texts. You may find activities inapplicable to your particular student population, but I hope what I present prompts you to think about ways to extend, modify, supplement, or inspire your own good ideas. As most teachers know, teaching is more like alchemy than an exact science, thus sharing my experiences is meant to exhibit the possibilities of what can be accomplished with graphic novels in the classroom rather than as a prescriptive set of instructions.

Each chapter in this book invites you into my classroom with student commentary, dialogue, or example work samples, followed by an overview of the graphic novel under study and its teachable topics, concepts, and skills. Most chapters contain reader response activities, examples of online student commentary, and a report on various classroom discussions. The material used in lessons explicated within the chapters can be found on the companion website, including additional student examples, study guides, discussion questions, quiz and test prompts, project directions, class activities, and assessments, along with links to audio and video files, author interviews, and other websites used as part of teaching units. It is not necessary to read each chapter sequentially, but it will be helpful to begin reading Part I first if you are unfamiliar with teaching visual literacy.

Visual Literacy

When I use the term *visual literacy* in this book, I mean the ability to interpret, negotiate, and make meaning from information presented in the form of an image, as well as to produce visual messages.

Chapter 1 focuses on ideas for teaching Scott McCloud's *Understanding Comics* (1993) where the emphasis is on fun, collaborative, constructive learning activities to teach concepts of visual literacy. Students learn a new vocabulary of the language of comics and develop criteria for evaluating comics and graphic novels as a method of effective storytelling. Through understanding the concept of closure, students realize and evaluate the role and influence of prior knowledge and experience in interpreting images and stories. They learn about making inferences, metacognition, and their role as active, constructive participants in the reading process.

Metacognition

When I use the term *metacognition* or *metacognitive* in this book, I intend it to mean thinking about one's own mental processes.

In Chapter 2, students are taught to break out of the preconditioned behavior of finding one right answer (Blau, 2003) when interpreting images from a chapter in Shaun Tan's all-graphic novel, *The Arrival* (2006). The lessons and activities show how making meaning occurs through collaboration and discussion. The second half of the chapter is a picture of students engaging in new graphic novel reading behavior as they explore Rachel Masilimani's "Two Kinds of People" (2007) and Gene Luen Yang's *American Born Chinese* (2008). Not only do students examine their own metacognition and perception when it comes to reading graphic texts, they explore self-perception as a theme in both of these works about racial identity.

Chapter 3 demonstrates a more traditional, literary approach to teaching Will Eisner's graphic novels, *A Contract With God* (2006a) and *A Life Force* (2006b) in which students engage with big picture questions about the universal human condition and develop criteria for assessing good literature. An argument activity over the primacy of words or pictures is exhibited, as well as online discussion about reading images. The chapter shows attention to traditional aspects of story, including character, theme, conflict, and setting, and through closer examination of story structure, students consider the relationship between form and content. The lessons in this chapter show how Eisner's stories foster rereading, deeper comprehension, success, and enjoyment for students.

Chapter 4 focuses on the genre of memoir, using Marjane Satrapi's *Persepolis* (2004, 2005). Through reading and writing, students realize the inherent challenges of writing from memory. A lesson featuring model excerpts from Mary Karr (2005, 2009) is used to teach students techniques of writing memoir using visual imagery and appealing to the five senses. Students compose visual memoir projects, and the chapter includes a vivid student sample graphic memoir. This chapter also shows students working on developing critical media literacy skills, expanding global perspectives, and examining gender and stereotypes. Example responses also show how students read and respond to *Persepolis* as a coming-of-age story.

Critical Media Literacy

When I refer to *critical media literacy,* I am referring to the Partnership for 21st Century Skills (2009) definition of analyzing media: Understanding both how and why media messages are constructed, and for what purposes, and examining how individuals interpret messages differently, how values and points of view are included or excluded, and how media can influence beliefs and behaviors. Students also apply a fundamental understanding of the ethical and legal issues surrounding the access and use of media. Critical media literacy also means creating media products; understanding and utilizing the most appropriate media creation tools, characteristics and conventions; and understanding and effectively utilizing the most appropriate expressions and interpretations in diverse, multicultural environments.

Chapter 5 again involves memoir, this time in a father-son thematic unit including Scott Russell Sanders's essay, "Under the Influence" (1989) and Elie Wiesel's *Night* (2006), taught as precursors to Art Spiegelman's *Maus* (1986, 1991). You will see students looking at and commenting on realism, expressionism, iconography, allegory, and the ways Spiegelman expands and plays with the graphic novel medium and stretches the boundaries of memoir. You will see students grappling with the importance and difficulty in representing the truth and the past through art and making connections between imagery in writing and graphic imagery in comics. Students improve comprehension through close reading and analysis, beginning with a set of quizzes for *Maus I,* and collaborate to build shared interpretations of *Maus II* using ICT skills. At the end of Chapter 5, students' heartfelt letters to Art Spiegelman illustrate the ways students make close personal connections to literature.

ICT Skills

When I use the ICT acronym, this refers to the *information, communications, and technology* definition from the Partnership for 21st Century Skills (2009). Quoting the framework definitions, applying technology effectively means using technology as a tool to research, organize, evaluate, and communicate information. It means using digital technologies, communication and networking tools, and social networks appropriately to access, manage, integrate, evaluate, and create information to successfully function in a knowledge economy, as well as to apply a fundamental understanding of the ethical and legal issues surrounding the access and use of information technologies.

In Chapter 6, students receive a glimpse into the world of Frank Miller's darker rendition of Batman by reading *Batman: The Dark Knight Returns* (2002). Practicing good reading strategies prompted by active and creative reader response activities, students persist through a difficult text filled with intertextual references, visually complex artwork, and a challenging panel layout.

Intertextual

When I use the word *intertextual* or *intertextuality* in this book, I mean the relationship that exists between different texts, especially literary texts, or the reference in one text to others.

The chapter also shows how students collaborate to write analytical essays or superhero narratives and includes a stunning student example. Through graphic novel and film study in this chapter, students are exposed to the superhero genre and examine the themes of justice, vigilantism, and the influence of the media in contemporary culture while developing English language arts and other twenty-first century skills.

The final chapter begins with a snapshot of a lesson that gets students on their feet and moving around the classroom, fostering interaction with text, rereading, discussion, and discovery of cultural and literary allusion in Alan Moore and David Lloyd's *V for Vendetta* (1988). Students examine Book II of *V for Vendetta* using Plato's Allegory of the Cave as a frame and collaborate to problem solve through challenging reading and to sustain focus through ambiguity. Independent discussion online about justice, morality, icons, heroes, and violence is exhibited, and application of concepts from *Understanding Comics* (1993) is applied in lessons given in this chapter. Students' quiz responses show analytical paragraph writing practice, and a number of writing response prompts are given. This chapter merely scratches the surface of teachable aspects of the very rich and complex *V for Vendetta*.

The final pages of this book leave you with some powerful, personal reflections from students in the graphic novel classroom, followed by resources for teaching graphic novels and a list of additional titles suitable for teaching in the secondary level classroom.

Creating Your Own Graphic Novel Classroom

I am extraordinarily lucky to teach an entirely graphic novels–based curriculum, and I understand that this is not the norm for most language arts teachers. As I listen to ideas from other teachers about the things they do in their classrooms, I always have my own students in mind in order to take away anything I find useful and exciting to do in my own classroom. I hope that this will be your approach to reading this book. Perhaps something in the individual chapters or on the companion website will help you plan lessons for your own students or supplement your current curriculum. Maybe the Resources or References will provide you with reading for further professional development and encourage you to join the discussion about graphic novels and twenty-first century teaching methodologies currently in progress. I hope this book shows preservice teachers a realistic picture of a classroom and offers insight about the importance of listening to students and creating a positive learning environment. I also hope it offers you generally applicable activities and ideas for teaching reading, writing, or integrating technology into traditional literature lessons. Maybe this book will prompt you to reflect on pedagogy or motivate you to take risks in your classroom to keep things fresh for yourself and students alike. I hope it convinces you that visual literacy as part of language arts development is valuable and legitimate for the next generation of students. For graphic novel teachers, I really hope this book confirms what you already do and provides you with a sense of collegiality. If you are new to the world of comics or graphic novels and have been open-minded enough to read this far, I hope this book encourages you to add them to your current ELA repertoire.

Part I

Looking at Literacy in the Graphic Novel Classroom

THERE IS NO LIFE HERE
EXCEPT THAT WHICH YOU
GIVE TO IT.

Page 59, panel 2, from *Understanding Comics* by Scott McCloud, copyright © 1993, 1994 by Scott McCloud. Reprinted by permission of HarperCollins.

1 Looking at the Comics Medium

Scott McCloud's *Understanding Comics*

"Today, you guys are going to work in groups. Once you get into groups, elect once person to sit in the hallway. You'll each get a scenario that the remainder of your group must draw together. You cannot add any words to your drawing! The person you elected to leave the classroom will return when every group is done drawing their scenario on the whiteboard, and this person will try to describe his or her team's scenario with words. The group whose member provides the most accurate description of his or her group's scenario wins! Group 1, here's your scenario: a blind man mowing his lawn while his seeing-eye dog relaxes in a hammock. Group 2: a hippie fish protesting a polluted lake. Group 3: . . ."

—Ms. Bakis

James Sturm's "Think Before You Ink" game is one of the fun, constructive activities I use in the graphic novel classroom to engage students in learning about how to use pictures to communicate and to reinforce the aspects of visual literacy found in Scott McCloud's *Understanding Comics* (1993). If you want to learn how to read a graphic novel by understanding the ins and outs of the comics medium, McCloud is the place to begin, though I also highly recommend Will Eisner's *Graphic Storytelling and Visual Narrative* (2008), especially if you are new to graphic novels or are teaching younger students. Eisner provides excellent background in storytelling basics, visual storytelling, the notion of empathy, and use of stereotypes. The reading assessment I use with my students for this text is provided at the companion website (www.corwin.com/graphic novelclassroom) and highlights the main ideas and concepts about comics and storytelling I like my students to become familiar with before reading graphic novels.

I teach Scott McCloud's *Understanding Comics* to help students understand and develop an appreciation for the important role of graphic art, visuals, and other media as communicative tools, as well as to more consciously realize their own role as constructive readers and communicators. McCloud reinforces the interdependent relationship of images and words that prompts students to get beyond the stereotypical perception of the role of images in graphic novels as supplementary or in service to a more important story told in words. *Understanding Comics* is also a useful tool in helping students exercise visual literacy while reading graphic novels and develop a critical language to better evaluate them beyond their literary merit. Understanding the relationship between form and content is crucial, which is why we begin with McCloud.

TEACHABLE TOPICS, CONCEPTS, AND SKILLS

Table 1.1 highlights important topics and skills associated with teaching Scott McCloud's *Understanding Comics*.

FRAMING THE TEXT

I engage students in *Understanding Comics* by presenting background about Scott McCloud using a TED Talk video featuring the author (McCloud, 2005). Using the interactive whiteboard to project our course social network site, I also bring students to McCloud's website (www .scottmccloud.com) to read his interactive, online comics narrative called "My Number" and his blog, to look at his work for Google, and to peruse the other resources available to aid their understanding of comics throughout the unit.

Since this is a nonfiction, information-heavy text, as students read chapters of *Understanding Comics*, I ask them to respond to study guide questions for homework to gauge their initial, independent comprehension of concepts before reviewing and applying them in class activities. The study guide is located at the companion website.

Table 1.1 Teachable Topics, Concepts, and Skills in Scott McCloud's *Understanding Comics*

Topics and Concepts	Skills
Iconography	Visual literacy
Closure	Reading comprehension (nonfiction)
Comics defined and sequential art	Acquiring and using new vocabulary
Understanding media	Awareness of reading process
Storytelling	Active, constructive reading
Human communication	Discussion
Consciousness of audience	Illustration and drawing
Panels	Metacognition
Panel transitions	Applying new concepts
Gutters	Identifying comics concepts
Bleeds	Problem solving
Balance of pictures and words in comics	Critical viewing
Time, sound, and motion in comics	Critical reading
The picture plane	Analysis
Art defined and the artistic process	Critical thinking and evaluation
Comparison of Eastern and Western comics	Making inferences
Color and comics	Making comparisons
Lines, emotions, and expressionism	Examining assumptions and preconceptions
Blurring	Drawing conclusions
Zip lines	Collaboration and cooperative learning
Streaking	Innovation and creativity

Defining Comics

We begin our classroom exploration of Chapter 1 of *Understanding Comics* by reviewing McCloud's brief history of comics, which is based on the way he defines the medium:

My students' compare their initial understanding of how they personally define comics with McCloud's definition, noting similarities and differences. Like the initial J. P. Toomey TED Talk video (2010), McCloud's broad definition helps to show students that comics encompass far more than what they initially determined in their original definitions. Making sure students understand the meaning of *aesthetic* (McCloud, 1993, p. 9) is critical in understanding McCloud's definition, as well as emphasizing the fact that

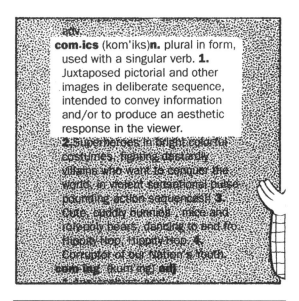

Page 9, panel 5, from *Understanding Comics* by Scott McCloud, copyright © 1993, 1994 by Scott McCloud. Reprinted by permission of HarperCollins.

McCloud does not use the term *words* in his definition. Contrasting the meaning of *aesthetic* with its opposite, *anesthetic,* is one way to do this, for it allows students to put their new knowledge into terms already familiar. Just as empathy is an important part of how readers relate to story, so too is aesthetic response vital in reading sequential art. McCloud later explains in Chapter 2 how words are part of the "other images" (p. 9) given in his comics definition by calling words abstract icons. To emphasize this aspect of the definition, I draw the same example McCloud gives on page 46 in panels 4 and 5 on the whiteboard for students. Contrasting the definition of comics McCloud provides with definitions of genre and art is another important part of teaching Chapter 1 of *Understanding Comics*. Magnifying the illustration of the water pitcher on page 6, panel 1, is a good way to display this concept clearly for students. Because students often confuse comics as another genre of literature, the distinction is important. Jessica Abel and Matt Madden's *Drawing Words & Writing Pictures* (2008) provides an excellent explanation of comics as a medium that also may be useful for classroom instruction.

LOOKING AT REPRESENTATION, ICONS, AND IDENTITY

Representation is a key concept in Chapter 2 of *Understanding Comics* and is shown most clearly in McCloud's famous "The Treachery of Images"

(p. 24–25) example, where the degree to which an idea or object is represented influences the reader's ability to comprehend its meaning. Also in Chapter 2, the distinction between abstract ideas and sensory objects is important in understanding the variety of ways artists convey story using these tools. The reader's participation in meaning-making by recognizing and interpreting the manner in which a person, place, thing, or idea is conveyed using lines and space is another important concept in Chapter 2. To reinforce McCloud's definition of icon on page 27, my students draw realistic and more iconic representations of themselves, as well as symbolic representations, during class (see below). Students draw examples on the whiteboard and we discuss levels of abstraction.

An alternative lesson might be to display various examples of icons in a slideshow presentation and have students answer aloud to which category each belongs, or students might search online for visual images and categorize them according to McCloud's definitions.

Participation: How Much of You Is in What You See?

The image on page 36 of *Understanding Comics* refers to reader participation, insofar as we see ourselves and extend our identities into iconic images. According to McCloud, this is a typically human response and part of the way we give meaning to what we see. My students are especially intrigued by this concept and connect it to the idea of empathy previously introduced in Eisner's *Graphic Storytelling and Visual Narrative.*

The less defined the images (the more cartoony), the better able we are to see ourselves or impose ideas and visions of ourselves into such a broadly defined image. McCloud proposes that this also gives us an opportunity to fantasize and play with such conjured visions of ourselves. Another way to understand this is to think of it as the way in which comics art invites readers to be "in" the story, therefore fostering more intimate engagement with the text. Abbey's understanding of this concept is evident in her reading response below:

> Cartoon faces are generalized, so that they could represent anybody. It makes it easy for the audience to insert themselves into the story, which amplifies the overarching meaning of the story. A character drawn too specifically is too distant from the audience.

Page 36, panel 4, from *Understanding Comics* by Scott McCloud, copyright © 1993, 1994 by Scott McCloud. Reprinted by permission of HarperCollins.

The degree of empathy depends on how intimately connected the reader feels to what he or she sees while reading. If we can imagine ourselves in a broadly defined image, chances are greater that we will feel as though we are in the story, a technique comics artists regularly exploit. My hope is that students will learn to exploit this technique in their own compositions as well.

Teaching Metacognition

I use McCloud's notion of identity to prompt students' awareness of their important participation in constructing meaning from graphic narrative and as an opportunity to explicitly teach students about metacognition. Some of the most important questions to ask students who are reading graphic novels include:

- What are you doing when you read comics?
- What cognitive processes are at work as you view images?
- Are you processing an image of an object or an idea?
- How do the various types of icons relate to one another?
- How does an icon convey meaning?

- How much of the meaning you interpret comes from you?
- How do the pictures and words work together to make meaning?

Answering such questions is difficult for students at first because they must consciously slow down while they read and reflect on their cognitive habits. Often students believe their lack of comprehension is due to stupidity rather than a lack of understanding of the reading process. So many thought processes occur while reading that it is challenging to consciously think about and name them, but if students can become more aware of their mental processes and behaviors, they can apply strategies to develop and strengthen good reading habits.

LOOKING AT CLOSURE

To understand McCloud's notion of closure in Chapter 3 of *Understanding Comics*, I ask students to explain it using *their own words*, then I ask them to draw. In my experience, students often memorize vocabulary without really thinking about the term or concept and its application, then regurgitate it for a quiz or test, only to forget the word soon after.

Here are some student definitions of closure:

"Being aware of the 'big picture' even though you can only see small fragments of it; you use your life experiences to piece them together."

—Kailey

"Filling the gaps between what we observe with perceptive faith of what is not observed."

—Jane

"Closure equals assuming."

—Jake

"Closure is observing something(s) and not actually taking everything but still understand it because of past experiences."

—Kaitlin

"The ability to complete a whole story by adding details to individually given parts."

—Danny

"Closure is when you may not see, hear, or physically sense what's there, but you know and assume it is."

—Shayna

Jane's drawings exhibit her understanding of closure and gutters as part of our Chapter 3 class activity. The lesson template is located at the companion website.

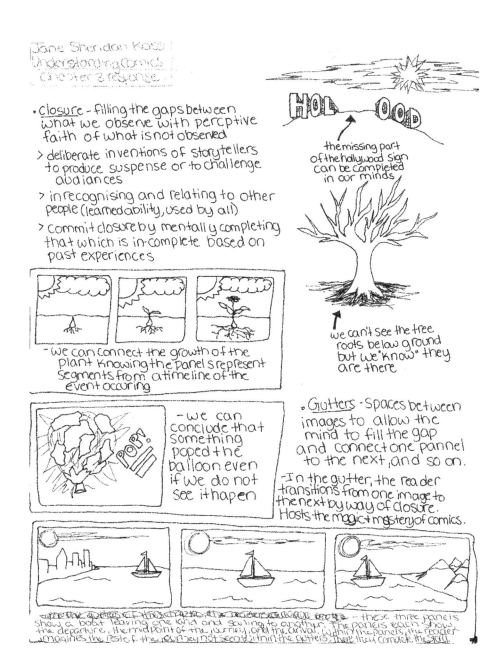

Josh and Abbey's drawings also illustrate their understanding of closure and gutters.

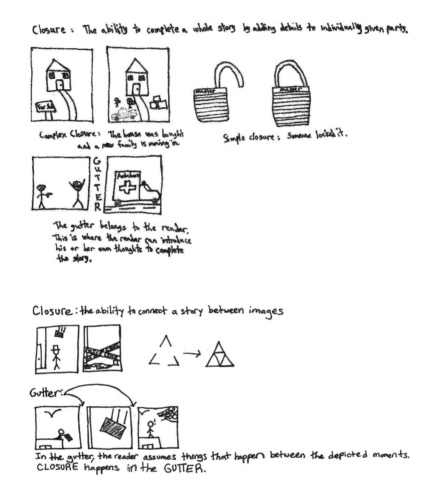

Constructive Reading in the Gutter

The gutter is the small space between panels where the reader must make necessary assumptions about images and commit closure to gain meaning. It is important for students to be conscious of their exact contribution when they look at the space between panels while reading comics. The conscious collaboration to which McCloud refers is a tremendous opportunity for students to understand themselves as readers, thinkers, and emotive human persons, including the prior knowledge and experience they bring to bear on what they see and what they do not see. It's also an opportunity to have more fun drawing! See the following student examples from a lesson reinforcing the notion of closure through drawing panel transitions.

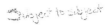

Transition: Action to Action

The final portion of the Chapter 3 lesson asks students to think about McCloud's title, *Understanding Comics: The Invisible Art,* as it relates to the idea of closure. In addition to interpreting the visible, the invisible is the portion of comics where the reader completes meaning as informed by prior knowledge and experience. Helping students become aware of their participation is the most important point of the lesson.

Connecting Understanding Comics to Writing Instruction

McCloud says on page 85 of *Understanding Comics* that comics artists make assumptions about readers' experiences, which is a great opportunity for teachers to raise the importance of audience in connection to composition instruction. One of the major flaws in students' writing is a lack of concern for the reader. When constructing an essay or any other form of writing, students often make unwarranted assumptions about their reader's level of knowledge or experience. Because students so often write to please the teacher and typically write *only* to the teacher as audience, they make far too many assumptions about the teacher's experience and insight into a text, often leading to a dearth of details or reasonable explanations in their writing. Additionally, if the student-teacher relationship is such that the teacher is perceived as authoritative with all the "correct" answers, often students feel like they have nothing to say that the teacher doesn't already know. This is why it is important to base discussion and assessment of literature on students' personal experience with the text, where they can be original about their reactions and prove their opinions using evidence from the text, including an understanding of its formal aspects. Chapter 3 of *Understanding Comics* presents an excellent place to help students see not only their active, constructive role in the reading process but also in their role as writers.

LOOKING AT TIME, SOUND, AND MOTION

McCloud explicates the various techniques implemented to handle the movement of time in comics in Chapter 4 of *Understanding Comics*. Learning about how time passes to retain reader engagement in sequential art narrative is important. If a story moves too slowly, readers will disengage, quickly become bored, or have an otherwise difficult or frustrating reading experience. If the pace is too rapid, readers become confused or lost among unclear relationships between panels. Students begin to understand the tools of time, sound, and motion that comics artists implement and better understand the formal aspects and language of comics when they apply these skills in fun, constructive class activities. While students find reading *Understanding Comics* challenging, they look forward to coming to class to draw and play games related to comics concepts. For our Chapter 4 activities, I ask students to draw time passing using sound in one panel, using McCloud's model panel on page 95, and draw time passing using multiple panels containing sound and motion, using model panels on pages 97 through 101 of *Understanding Comics.* I also implement activities for exercising understanding of time, sound, and motion found at www.teachingcomics.org, many of which elicit excitement, creativity, and laughter.

LOOKING AT LINES, EMOTION AND THE INVISIBLE

The relationship between lines and emotions in Chapter 5 presents an opportunity for students to discuss aesthetic responses while reading images. My students report that images cause in them a more immediate response than words, and they especially enjoy that part of reading graphic novels. Before viewing a PowerPoint presentation in class that highlights important examples of concepts in Chapter 5, I ask students to draw one emotion on paper as a warm-up activity. Providing students with a list of emotions might be necessary or helpful. Drawing the intangible challenges students in a fun way, and by trying their hand at it, they develop a more thorough appreciation for the representation of God and other abstractions in the graphic novels they read. Eisner's use of the window and the weather to represent God in *A Contract With God* (2006a) is one example of the "invisible" that students immediately recognized after learning about the invisible aspect of comics.

LOOKING AT THE BALANCE OF PICTURES AND WORDS

The spectrum of combinations of words and pictures McCloud explains in Chapter 6 of *Understanding Comics* affords students a fun opportunity to draw various examples of their own. Using McCloud's examples of how words alone allow an artist to be creative with the pictures and vice versa on pages 157 through 159 as a model, half the students in class might create written mini-scripted stories first and then play with the pictures to complete their graphic narrative, while the rest of the students draw an all-visual story first and play with adding words next. I require my students apply their understanding of McCloud's picture-word combinations to their reading of Book II in *V for Vendetta* (Moore & Lloyd, 1988), but identifying word and image combinations is a lesson that can be applied to any graphic narrative.

   You also might reinforce McCloud's picture and word combinations using a lesson called Practicing Text-Image Relationships by Christian Hill (n.d.) found at www.teachingcomics.org. This is a fun activity that takes about 20 to 30 minutes to complete and discuss with students. Additionally, I also have students add captions to the images in the *New Yorker* caption contest found at the back of each issue, another enjoyable activity. Both of these mini-lessons provide much needed laughter and help students persist through the rather dense *Understanding Comics*.

LOOKING AT ART AND COLOR

Chapter 7 of *Understanding Comics* invites students to think critically about McCloud's definition of art and the artistic process. His interpretation initiates interesting dialogue among students about the definition of art (their own in comparison to McCloud's), as well as the role of art in culture and art's influence on humanity. For those students who do not see writing or dance as an art and are limited in their understanding of art as strictly graphic forms, like painting or drawing, this proves a valuable topic. Just as McCloud's definition of comics broadens students' initial understanding of comics, so too did his interpretation of art—that is, "any human activity which doesn't grow out of either of our species two basic instincts: survival and reproduction" (p. 164).

Chapter 8 presents an opportunity for students to talk about their aesthetic response to reading color. As is true with everything readers see, colors carry associations based on prior knowledge and experience. I have used the common psychology of color lesson that many teachers are familiar with to discuss the effects of color on reading comics. A simple warm-up activity that you might try with students is to ask, what color are you, or if you were a color, what color would you be? It is certainly useful for students to review the various associations and conventional meaning of color and the role color plays in adding further dimension to understanding graphic narrative. Many of the students involved in graphic arts were especially intrigued by Chapters 7 and 8, as is evident in Stephen's blog comment:

> I had a tremendously interesting reading experience yesterday. I had just read Chapter 7 of Scott McCloud's *Understanding Comics*, which partly dealt with the way great art is a balance between the basics of form and message. I personally loved this idea, and reading such an in-depth and well thought-out deconstruction of the artistic process really got me thinking about my own writing in a more critical way. Later that day, and as a direct result of my research project, I checked Neil Gaiman's *Sandman* out of the library. As I was reading it, I was immediately reminded

of that same balance. In *Sandman*, Gaiman uses decidedly non-traditional form to tell a complex, original story in a world of dreams. One of the more notable examples of this is a sequence detailing a young women's prophetic dream, which is formatted in a landscape form, forcing the reader to literally hold and read the comic differently from the rest of the story. This provides a great feeling of "otherness" and surrealism to this section, which I enjoyed intensely and it immediately reminded me of McCloud's balance of message and form.

VISUAL LITERACY, MEDIA, AND COMMUNICATION

Though *Understanding Comics* requires extra attention to comprehend new concepts and vocabulary associated with comics, students can still make personal connections to the work, especially through reflection on and discussion of Chapter 9. "Putting It All Together" presents a final opportunity for students to see the relevance of understanding not only comics but all media in their own efforts to communicate and their ability to read and appreciate stories. This is where I begin to discuss why reading graphic novels is a worthwhile endeavor. The chapter not only reinforces the connection between form and meaning in art, but it lends itself beautifully to a discussion of human communication, which lies at the heart of teaching English language arts (ELA).

Within Chapter 9, I focus closely on pages 193 to 198 to emphasize the ways that human beings try to understand one another. McCloud describes this important aspect of human nature and speaks directly to the various modes and means available to understand ourselves and our humanity.

We all live in a state of ***profound isolation***. No other human being can ever know what it's like to be you from the inside. And no amount of ***reaching out*** to ***others*** can ever make them feel exactly what ***you*** feel. All media of communication are a ***by-product*** of our sad ***inability*** to communicate ***directly*** from ***mind to mind.*** Sad, of course, because nearly all problems in human history ***stem*** from that inability. Each ***medium*** (the term comes from the Latin word meaning ***middle***) serves as a bridge ***between*** minds. Media convert thoughts into forms that can transverse the ***physical world*** and be ***re***-converted by one or more senses ***back*** into thoughts. In comics the conversion follows a path from mind to hand to paper to eye to mind. Ideally the artist's "message" will run this gauntlet without being affected by it, but in practice this is rarely the case. (193–198)

Our class discussion focuses on McCloud's very powerful words centered on how often conflict arises from failure to communicate effectively. Students make strong personal connections to their own experiences by relaying their feelings about being misunderstood by parents, friends, or teachers. They also talk about the difficulties involved with putting the ideas in their heads into words and putting words on paper. This chapter presents an excellent opportunity to discuss with students the connection between formal education, literacy practice, and their personal concerns. Helping students make the connection between language and their own humanity is done best through teaching stories and is such an important part of our job as literacy teachers.

The following additional questions may be useful to write or blog about online or for small or large group discussion.

- What are the various forms of communication (media) that human beings use to communicate?
- *Briefly* explain how each media you named above works to convey meaning.
- How many of those media do *you use* and for what *purpose* or to what end?
- What kind of meaning do *comics* (as McCloud defines it) convey?
- What criteria or standards will you use to find meaning in the graphic novels we plan to read this year?
- What are the most important concepts you learned from McCloud that will inform your reading of graphic novels?

Looking at Assessment

In addition to assessing students' reading and thinking by way of journal responses and reviewing and applying concepts during class activities, I have my students read Chris Ware's "Unmasked," a short graphic narrative from *The New Yorker* (2009), and respond to twelve questions designed to test their ability to apply various concepts learned in *Understanding Comics*. Located at the companion website, the test can be easily modified and applied to a graphic narrative of your choice or an excerpt from a longer graphic novel.

Another idea for assessing students' knowledge of comics is to have students create their own graphic narrative utilizing the various concepts introduced in *Understanding Comics*. Many students are uncomfortable with drawing for a grade, but designing rubrics that stress process rather than product can allay students' fears and perhaps your own! I give my students a choice to work with a partner to illustrate their understanding of comics in a graphic narrative composition project. Like writing, students really do gain greater appreciation and deeper understanding of the medium by attempting to compose in it. Comics are famous for their collaborative nature, so I encourage students to work together to create stories. Examples of students' comics can be found in the chapters that follow.

LOOKING AT STUDENTS' RESPONSE TO READING *UNDERSTANDING COMICS*

The following excerpts from their blogs show how students feel about reading Scott McCloud's *Understanding Comics*.

> "I'm finally starting to enjoy this class more. When school first started I didn't really look forward to it because I never liked comics since I found them confusing and hard to follow. After reading McCloud, I think I'm able to understand them better and appreciate them as a medium. While Understanding Comics wasn't exactly the most exciting book, I'm glad we read it because it definitely makes reading other comics more enjoyable."
>
> —Katie

> "After reading scott mcclouds book understanding comics i feel that i have a much better understanding of the comics medium and the tools they use to get their point across. i wasnt aware of what the gutters purpose was nor was i aware of the way graphic novelists utilized icons to represent abstract ideas or emotions. the book also helped me understand the importance of lines in a comic and the many different ideas they can represent such as motion and smell. the book was confusing but it really helped a lot.
>
> —Mike

> "Understanding comics shows how much work is put into making and understanding graphic novels. During class trying to draw certain actions is harder than it looks. The way you draw a certain line can change how you interpret the image completely.

Id rather be reading an actual graphic novel with a story base then Scott McClouds Understanding Comics. But it does give good insight."

—Jen Yeo

CONCLUSION

Through McCloud, my students learn about formal aspects of a medium of communication, as well as considering the relevance of communication in their own lives. Reading *Understanding Comics* also leads to a richer understanding and appreciation for the comics artists' work in graphic novels. Newly acquired knowledge of comics also enables students to develop a clearer, more specific and detailed criteria for judging a "good" graphic novel, one based on more than a surface reaction to plot or other purely literary concerns. When students are introduced to the language of comics, its vocabulary, grammar, and purpose, their understanding can lead them to both a deeper understanding of story and their own personal experiences reading and writing. As you will see in the chapters ahead, visual literacy and perception are both directly applicable skills and thematic in many graphic novels students read in the graphic novel classroom.

2 Interpreting Images

Shaun Tan's *The Arrival*
Rachel Masilimani's *Two Kinds of People*
Gene Luen Yang's *American Born Chinese*

"Sometimes people see things that they want to see or things that aren't actually there, especially when it comes to racial stereotypes."

—Laura Murphy

aura's comment pertains to her beliefs about racial stereotypes as part of her response to students' online discussion forum about the themes in Gene Luen Yang's *American Born Chinese* (2008), but her statement also describes more generally the ways in which we read and interpret. Often students read into a text, drawing unwarranted conclusions because of their conditioning in a traditional academic setting. Kenny confirms such habits of reading in his portfolio reflection:

> I have developed a rather unfortunate form of reading. I read to write. In other words, I read a novel and scan for things I can use in an essay, or scan for symbols that I will be tested on. This distracts me from what is actually happening on those pages. I have had the standard 5 paragraph essay format, and the strategies to identify symbols crammed down my throat. I read to do well in a class, not for the usual reading pleasures like entertainment, information, and support.

For a long time, students have been trained to find the answers in a text and report them to their teacher, but in this chapter, you will see a graphic novel classroom in which students are reoriented to a more democratic approach to literacy and learning. Learning to look at images, read them in sequence, and comprehend their meaning in an active and constructive way is meant to transform the way students understand the reading process and themselves as critical thinkers. This is best accomplished with good graphic narratives and twenty-first century pedagogy.

TEACHABLE TOPICS, CONCEPTS, AND SKILLS

Table 2.1 Teachable Topics, Concepts, and Skills in *The Arrival*, "Two Kinds of People," and *American Born Chinese*

Topics and Concepts	Skills
Perception	Perception
Stereotypes (exaggerated, negative, and racial), labels and categorization	Active, constructive reading
Hyperbole	Rereading
Mood	Visual literacy (reading images in sequence)
Diction	Metacognition
Closure (as defined by Scott McCloud)	Listening
Metaphor	Oral and online discussion
Characterization	Collaboration
Film technique	Social meaning-making
Identity and social conformity	Examining preconceptions and assumptions
Immigration	Problem solving
Controversial images	Critical analysis
Reading as process	Defending an interpretation (using textual and other support)
Spectrum of interpretation (relativism, absolutism)	Writing an argument or persuasive essay
Reading "into" a text, misreading	Recognizing and applying prior knowledge

Topics and Concepts	Skills
Metacognition and self-awareness	
Popular culture allusions	
Writing a thesis	
Defending a position in writing using textual support	

I use an excerpt from Shaun Tan's all-graphic novel, *The Arrival* (2006), to teach students about the influence of prior knowledge and experience on interpretation, especially when reading images. I teach Rachel Masilimani's short graphic narrative, "Two Kinds of People" (2007), and Gene Luen Yang's graphic novel, *American Born Chinese* (2008), in tandem to examine labels, stereotypes, and issues surrounding identity relevant to teenagers, as well as to emphasize the transactional nature of reading with students, encouraging them to begin exploring and experiencing texts rather than scouring them for answers to test questions. Students feel accomplished when reading these texts, for their brevity allows them to read and enjoy an entire story without interruption, and the sophisticated conversation that these stories provoke (and the skills teachers can emphasize) prevents students from feeling the texts are overly simplistic or dumbed down because they are graphic.

The activities and guided reading response questions for each story in this chapter are designed to make students aware of their own interpretive abilities and developing visual literacy skills, rather than to impede a pleasurable reading experience or focus on plot-related details. I encourage students to begin reading images as an important aspect of story, beyond cursorily looking at them as incidental to the words as they are typically accustomed.

LOOKING AT *THE ARRIVAL*

The Arrival is an entirely wordless story about a man who leaves his family in his homeland and arrives in a strange new place where he must adjust to his new surroundings. Though I use only Chapter 1 of *The Arrival* to strictly focus on form and skills, this graphic novel is valuable for teaching younger and older students about adventure, immigration, and immigration stories, and it is especially suited for engaging reluctant and English language learners. Excellent materials containing analysis and ways to use both *The Arrival* and *American Born Chinese* to explore immigrant identity and experiences are located at the companion website (www.corwin.com/graphicnovelclassroom).

Rationale

The rationale for teaching Tan's all-graphic text is its potential in helping students become better learners through metacognitive reflection, for the all-graphic text demands attention to self as reader as active participant rather than considering text as primary or superior. In the example lesson described below, students look, read, listen, reread, and revise original conclusions in an effort to derive meaning from the sequential images and build consensus. Because the images are open to interpretation, the ensuing discussion fosters collaboration, which helps build a community of readers. This lesson also demonstrates how reading is a constructive and process-oriented act requiring rereading and reconstruction, and therefore it might be taught as a precursor to teaching Scott McCloud's *Understanding Comics* (1993) or afterwards to reinforce closure and other concepts of visual literacy.

Objectives

The objectives of the lesson are for students to practice reading sequential art and images, write personal responses based on metacognitive reflection, and learn about how words add specific meaning when applied to sequential images. While students listen, discuss, and draw conclusions, they also reflect on learning and make connections between the process of reading and the process of writing.

Reading and Responding to Images

To begin, I ask students to independently look at the cover page and read through the end of Chapter 1 to make meaning. Since the text is comprised entirely of images, there is more room for interpretation, and this is its exact value in teaching students about themselves as readers and thinkers. Second, I ask students to individually answer journal questions focused primarily on a metacognitive reflection of their reading experience. This can be done in class or for homework.

Reader Response Prompts and Sample Student Response

Give a summary of the chapter. What is this excerpt about?

Ryan's Response: This chapter is about a man who is leaving his family. The story starts off with a bunch of faces which could possibly symbolize the faces of other people who have gone through a similar situation as he has. It is clear that the man is packing to leave his modest home and he then walks to the train station with his family. There is an ominous shadow in the back round of the next couple of pages, I believe that it looks like a dragon. I think that the picture is foreshadowing some sort of impending doom for the man and his family. The story ends with the man departing on the train to an unknown destination. I personally think he is leaving to find work or maybe start a better life in a new location. The last page is the man's wife and daughter walking back home alone with the dark shadow in the sky. There is no question in my mind that something bad is going to happen to this family due to all of the dark images in this story.

> Describe the mental processes you used to figure out what this story is about.

Ryan's Response: First I read through the story very quickly which was a terrible idea because I had no idea what it was about. The second time I read it a little slower. This helped a lot because it allowed me to catch certain details which I did not notice the first time I read the story. I noticed that the man is clearly leaving his family and that his wife and daughter were distraught. This then allowed me to make my own assumptions as to why he left his family. He could have possibly been looking for work or he may have been forced to leave due to persecution.

> Describe the mood of the piece.

Ryan's Response: The mood of this story is very sad and dark. The pictures are all drawn with the intent to make the reader feel some sort of empathy for the main character. I can honestly say that I did feel a little sad during this story, especially when the man's wife is crying at the end.

> What specific aspects of the visual images contribute to the mood?

Ryan's Response: The most obvious example of an image contributing to the mood is the image of the dark dragon like shadow in many of the pictures. The author could have chosen to put a rainbow in place of it but he chose to draw dark and scary clouds. It is obvious that the author wanted the mood to be dark.

> Give one example of film technique or angled shots in the chapter. Explain how this technique influences the meaning of the narrative/ story.

Ryan's Response: One technique which I thought was very interesting was early in the chapter. The author drew images of specific things like a clock, a picture and tea cup along with other random house objects. Then on the next page the author panned out and it showed the room where all of these objects were located in. It was a clever way for the author to show which objects had significance and were important.

> Choose a favorite or interesting or perplexing panel. Describe it using as much written detail as possible.

Ryan's Response: My favorite panel is the one where the man takes off his hat and under it is a origami bird. This is my favorite panel because it is slightly confusing. Why did the man have the bird under his hat? Also I can't help but wonder what the significance of this bird is. He did give it to his daughter as a parting gift however the bird did show up numerous other times in the story. I believe that the bird must have some other significance besides simply being a nice gift for his daughter.

Adding Words to Pictures

After students initially read and respond, I then require them to add words to the story as they read the text a second time during class. They receive little instruction about how to do this, except that they may write directly on their paper copy using speech and thought bubbles, as well as captions and other narration. Students are free to add words in any manner they deem appropriate. By adding words, students are essentially writing what they understand the text means to them. After students add words, I ask a few willing students to share their stories by reading the words they wrote, while classmates follow along using their own copies of the excerpt. I discourage students from prefacing their interpretations with commentary. They often try to add explanation about why they wrote what they did for fear of judgment or in an effort to explain their word choices based on their concern that it might lack clarity or be different from other students' answers. This is the very point of the lesson—to reassure them that their interpretations might be valid even if they differ from their peers.

After a number of students read, all students are then encouraged to comment on the differences or variety of interpretations in the stories they heard. I ask students to show by raising hands whether the story they just heard from a peer is the same as their interpretation. By default, those whose interpretations differ are asked to share their version by reading aloud. You might repeat this sequence one or two more times, depending on how much time you have in class. By sharing and listening to the way others' read the text and the variations in meaning, and by facilitating the discovery and discussion of those differences, students realize how much their own experiences and prior knowledge colors, influences, or otherwise affects their understanding, in this case of an excerpt from a graphic novel containing sequential images without words.

Defending Interpretations

I subsequently require students to defend their interpretations by asking them to point out exactly which images led them to particular conclusions or how they made meaning from individual images in context of the whole piece. Inevitably, students see images in portions of panels that others might not have recognized. The students realize at this point how "not seeing" can alter their understanding of a text. If the students do not discover this independently, the teacher can facilitate recognition through question and answer or explicit explanation. Scott McCloud's understanding of comics as "the invisible art" is realized in this lesson in two capacities: not seeing can lead to limited understanding or an incomplete interpretation, and "filling in" the meaning in a sequential art narrative comes from our prior experience, something that is invisible or external to the text but that we mentally add to make what we see and read more complete and meaningful. Learning to read an all-graphic text in this lesson is an effective way to teach students to read not only graphic narrative but all forms of media.

LOOKING FOR THE ONE RIGHT ANSWER

The variety of interpretations about the meaning of the text led students to ask, "Was the way I understood the story the right way?" Students almost always need the reassurance they got the right answer or that they did the correct thing. I respond to this question with another: "Is there one right answer? I also lead students to reevaluate their original conclusions by rereading and reconsidering (and reconstructing) the text in light of the new knowledge about how others read it. I think it is important for students to understand that rereading is necessary and a habit of good readers in the same way that good writers draft, revise, and edit (Blau,

2003). I don't recall students being as willing to go back to reassess traditional print text, most likely because of their length and the time it takes to reread sentences of print, but in this lesson and in others involving graphic novels, students had no problem flipping through the pages quickly and efficiently to review. In this case, brief quality learning trumps quantity of words. Often, students easily locate a particular image that might be a point of contention or discussion almost effortlessly from memory. Teaching students that they must be able to defend their interpretations by directly finding proof or cause for their conclusions in the text is important, and locating images quickly allows them to find their supporting evidence, important prewriting strategies.

The Spectrum of Interpretation

At the end of this lesson, I ask: What can we conclude from the way you and your classmates interpreted that story? Students respond about the different ways readers read and pictures being worth a thousand words, and then we discuss through a brief question-and-answer period how readers make meaning from an active transaction and participation with text. Discussion about authorial intent usually arises and we also raise the issue of misreading, misinterpretations, and "reading into" a text. To introduce the spectrum of interpretation, I propose the following questions for discussion with students.

- Can a text mean anything we want it to?
- Is authorial intent the actual meaning of a story?
- Is there one absolute and correct interpretation?
- Is meaning more fluid or more permanent?

The spectrum below is the visual I draw on the whiteboard for students to discuss, and it visually orients students to the variety of interpretation that exists when reading a text.

Absolute Meaning (one correct meaning) ----------- Relativism (text can mean anything we decide)

Looking at the spectrum leads us to further discussion about the role interpretation plays, not only in reading fictional texts, but in the sciences, social sciences, and law.

CONCLUSION

The most important reason I use this lesson using *The Arrival* is to immediately implement a pedagogical approach that many students are unfamiliar with—the elimination of the top-down model of teaching and engaging in a truly student-centered approach based on Louise Rosenblatt's transactional theory (1995). I introduce and repeatedly reinforce the notion that students must pay attention to themselves as readers, as well as the essential relevance of that role, to foster metacognitive reflection. I find myself repeating our mantra many times throughout this lesson: Tell me what you think, not what you think I want to hear! Since "unlocking the text" has been a traditional method of learning, students are predisposed to reading in prescribed ways and they are therefore often confused or resist my seemingly new expectations and the new environment. When students can no longer find the answers to a text's meaning on the Internet or wait to hear the teacher's interpretation, they instead must think critically on their own, trust their own conclusions, and be accountable for their own interpretations. This requires more overall participation in learning, which some students find painful. *The Arrival* lesson also fosters a sense of collaboration and highlights social meaning-making—the process of listening to others and revising one's own initial thinking based on this new information. As students begin to understand their more powerful role as interpreters rather than "finders of one right answer," their approach to reading changes and their enjoyment and appreciation of story increases.

LOOKING AT LABELS IN RACHEL MASILIMANI'S "TWO KINDS OF PEOPLE"

"The human mind likes patterns. It likes to generalize and categorize, because otherwise the world is too complex for comprehension. This applies to human interaction; just as we categorize plants and animals, we categorize each other. We create labels according to appearance and location and personality. For the most part, these labels are useful and generally accurate; however, they can be abused all too easily. For example, possessing a dual identity is nearly impossible within this system of labels. In the short story 'Two Kinds of People,' Rachel Masilamani recounts her experiences as an Indian-American teenager trying to fit herself into her own categorized world view. As the writer, Masilamani mixes a real world setting with fantastical and symbolic images to illustrate her real life conflict."

—Abbey

Abbey's essay introduction reflects the usefulness of using Rachel Masilimani's "Two Kinds of People" to help students realize the relationship between content and form. In addition to careful analysis of its sequential images and graphic style, "Two Kinds of People" spurs discussion about labels, stereotypes, and identity, and it serves as prereading for Yang's longer novel.

"Two Kinds of People" is about a teenager who tries to categorize herself and others in order to understand her identity in terms of how the rest of the world is organized. Unfortunately, she doesn't know which label to apply to herself, and as she is half German and half Indian, there is no clearly delineated "box" to check for her racial profile except for "other," which seems to suggest that unless a person can clearly identify themselves as either black or white, they matter less. Students found Masilimani's short story personally meaningful and relevant to their own lives, as indicated in Joshua's journal responses (see below). Abbey's essay excerpt above shows that though brief, "Two Kinds of People" provides rich topics for students to talk and write about. Questions for Rachel Masilimani's "Two Kinds of People" can be found in Robert Diyanni's *Literature: Reading Fiction, Poetry, and Drama* (Masilimani, 2007). Here is how Joshua responded to those questions in his journal:

1.) I think I can relate to some of the situations in two kinds of people. I am not a different ethnicity but when I was younger I had a lot of trouble reading and I was put into special ed classes. I was kind of embarrassed and I often felt that I stuck out. This was really apparent when I was pulled out of classes. The story itself is not just about the issue of ethnicity it is applicable to all of those who feel different from others.

2.) The central question of two kinds of people is how people are defined or grouped. When people looked at the Indian girls from the story they categorized them in their mind as being different, as not being the classic American. The story questions whether we should categorize people the way we do and the possible effects of categorizing others.

3.) Aspects of the culture come into the story with the stereotypes of the other girl from India and the gingerbread cookies that came out "just right". I think this added to the story because it in a way caused the reader to categorize in-spite of themselves and caused the reader to question even more the worth of categorizing.

5.) I think Masiliamani may have written this piece in an attempt to try to stop people from trying to define people further then just being people. Rather then defining race, sexual orientation, or intelligence it may be better to just accept people as people

6.) Stereotypes are defined images that evoke a usual classic response. It is important for us to know what a stereotype is because they are often used in comics as a matter of convenience. They make the story flow very quickly and they are easy to understand. A negative stereotype is a stereotype that evokes a response that defines the person in a way that is based on a untrue and hurtful misconception.

In addition to getting students further accustomed to reading and analyzing images and panels in Masilimani's shorter piece, the conflict over racial identity in the story also primes students for reading Gene Luen Yang's novel, *American Born Chinese*, in which students will discover and explore the relationship between meaning and form.

LOOKING AT *AMERICAN BORN CHINESE*

"After i finished reading *American Born Chinese* last week I came to realize that it is my favorite book i have read through out English at Masco. Not only did I enjoy it because it was an easier read then most books that I have read but the plot of the story intregued me. I liked how Gene Luen Yang made the creative transformation between the two characters. I would never have guessed that the story would end up that way."

—Aaron Palmer

"I think the art of the story was interesting, mainly because it's so different from what else we've read so far or, really, most of the other graphic novels I've seen; it's very cartoonish, but in a bolder, cleaner, more modern way than Eisner's work. There were times when the art felt almost childish—as with Jin's frequent 'jolts of confidence'—but that was partly offset by the positioning of the page. The large amounts of white space gave it a slightly more sophisticated feel, maybe partially because it was so different from a traditional comic book, in which the whole page would be filled with panels. I was also pretty fascinated by the way Yang played with the medium—it didn't happen too often, but the ironic sitcom laughter during Danny's story and the *Monkey King* breaking the panel in order to go outside the boundaries of reality were two examples. (The laugh track in particular gave that specific story a slightly more disturbing feel—the idea that people would react to offensive racial stereotypes with laughter as opposed to horror, and the fact that this imaginary audience laughs even at people openly mocking Chin-Kee made the story considerably more unsettling.)"

—Olivia Parks

As you can see from the divergent blog comments above, *American Born Chinese* is a graphic novel that appeals to a range of readers and provokes enjoyment and critical thinking. The novel is about the painful process of realizing the futility of denying one's identity, an experience most often created by the pressure of social conformity, and though the novel is primarily aimed at a middle school audience, my seventeen- and eighteen-year-old students laud *American Born Chinese* as a favorite for its themes and colorful format. My eleven-year-old daughter read and enjoyed it on her own without instruction, but I would argue that my older students more thoroughly enjoyed the story for having read it in school, where they were given the opportunity to ask questions, sort through confusions, share their individual interpretations, and socialize while discussing their reading experiences more communally. Another important reason to read *American Born Chinese* in the classroom is to guide students in deconstructing the exaggerated, negative stereotypes in the novel.

LOOKING AT CONTROVERSIAL IMAGES

The first time I taught *American Born Chinese*, I asked students to read the novel during class and discuss their reactions online in a social network discussion forum, which allowed students to discuss the sensitive racial issue in a fashion where they had ample time to think and carefully compose their comments. One Asian American student in my class reported that his participation in the online discussion provided a safe space to voice his important perspective about the character, Chin-Kee, without feeling that all eyes were literally on him. As is common experience when teaching novels that include racial stereotypes, like Mark Twain's *Adventures of Huckleberry Finn*, *American Born Chinese* demands adept skill from teachers in fostering healthy discussion in a carefully constructed classroom environment. This year, I observed that the handful of Asian American students did not participate orally in class at all as we discussed *American Born Chinese*, but instead voiced their opinions in their blog posts. Ali wrote:

This week we read *American Born Chinese* and I actually liked the book. I didn't find the book itself offensive at all, but rather the reactions people had to it. Some people thought that the book had no application to real life and that nobody resented their own heritage. The fact is, Asian is quite possibly the strangest race to belong to in the Tritown. There's almost none of us. I walk in limbo; being half white and half Asian, I can understand what Jin is going through. No matter how white you act, people will always assume that any grade you got or any talent you may have is because you are Asian. But, to tell the truth, I'm not even Asian really. My dad is the opposite of Asian stereotypes and I was pretty much only raised by my white mother. If I didn't have dark hair, nobody would even think I was Asian. In fact, Asians make fun of me for being white. I guess what I'm saying is that Asian is a race that people feel comfortable pointing out because they don't associate it with any sort of real racism as we do with African Americans, despite the fact that they too were victims of slavery. I guess what I'm trying to say is that Asian is just a weird area to be placed in.

Kevin wrote:

I thoroughly enjoyed American Born Chinese, because unlike most people in the class, I felt a real connection to the story. I am an American born Chinese kid, and have experienced a lot of what Jin Wang has gone through. I used to feel like I was Chin-Kee, the weird Asian kid that always attracted attention, so I tried to make myself a fly on the wall and reject my heritage. But as I grew older, I learned that no matter how hard I try, I will always be Chinese, and that is always how people will perceive me. So it doesn't make sense for me to even try to reject my Chinese heritage.

In addition to the discussion that occurs around the issue of racial stereotypes as embodied in the character of Chin-Kee, Danny's annoying cousin, the structure of *American Born Chinese* also draws ample attention from student readers. The separate yet intertwining plotlines challenge readers to sustain a bit of ambiguity while also prompting predictions about how the three stories are related, which is eventually revealed at the end of the story. The "twist" at the end of the novel is satisfying and rewarding to developing readers who have either persisted through a sustained period of not knowing or have been entertained long enough with the three plots to see what unfolds. Yang seems to have understood the ways young students read by keeping them engaged enough to stick with the story and rewarding them with a pleasing resolution. This is important to note since an unwillingness to persist through ambiguity and difficult reading is something that sends most students running to the Internet for answers or causes them to disregard reading altogether. Other aspects of the text, including the images of William Hung (p. 203) and the YouTube video of the Asian boys singing the Back Street Boys' song (back page), help students feel successful at identifying references to popular culture, which allows for further, deeper discussion of the importance, form and function of intertextuality, and allusion whether reading or writing texts.

LOOKING AT TEXTUAL CHALLENGES

Though seemingly simple because of its colorful, cartoony artwork, *American Born Chinese* can present challenges for the most competent readers. An example of the learning opportunities that can result from students' misreading became apparent in a whole class activity in which I asked groups of students to note specific examples from the text that they judged as most important images. Students also expressed their confusions in our online discussion forum. Laura wrote:

> For me, what made this novel so confusing was the way the author portrayed both symbolic and realistic images in a literal way. . . . for example, Jin Wang didn't literally change his physical appearence, it was all in his head, and yet for the rest of the book he was continuously portrayed as this new character, and even reffered to as "Danny".

Misinterpretation of the image on page 194 where the herbalists' wife appears in Jin Wang's dream also plagues students.

Some students interpreted the appearance of this woman literally, failing to realize she is part of Jin's dream, and inaccurately conclude that she causes Jin's transformation into Danny. This conclusion directly contradicts the inner turmoil that both Jin and the Monkey King wrestle with in terms of their futile attempts to alter their own identity as the central conflict of the novel. Some students make the incorrect assumption that the herbalist's wife is performing some sort of magic that causes Jin's physical change, incorrectly introducing the notion of an external force of change to the story. The importance of discussing particular images in context of the narrative—that is, explicitly examining the relationship among images—cannot be overstated. The misunderstanding that arises also emphasizes the crucial importance of reading images as part of the language of the narrative rather than as incidental to words.

Page 194 from *American Born Chinese* by Gene Luen Yang, copyright © 2008 by Gene Luen Yang. Reprinted by permission of Henry Holt.

The illustration of metaphorical and literal change that occurs in *American Born Chinese* is central to understanding the story, and the above example of misinterpretation shows the important role of the teacher in facilitating problem solving through collaboration. Dialogue among students about images and their interpretation, encouraging rereading, and focusing on the problematic aspects of text, as opposed to avoiding them or providing students with answers, is essential in students' positive reading experience and understanding of this graphic novel. Whereas some critics will argue that reading images is too open to interpretation, I would submit that this is exactly the power of images, for the learning opportunities they provide in a classroom setting under the direction of a skilled instructor.

LOOKING AT ONESELF AS READER

Since students can read *American Born Chinese* in less than two class periods, this leaves ample time to spend discussing the novel, resolving confusions, thinking critically about its formal features, and practicing writing skills. I also spend extra time teaching students to reflect on themselves as readers. To this end I post the following discussion question online for students to discuss for homework. Two sample students' responses follow.

Online Discussion Prompt and Sample Student Responses

> Discuss the nature of your reading experience of *American Born Chinese*. Write about your reactions, confusions, opinions, or insights. Feel free to begin your own discussion thread and invite others to comment. What experience or assumptions did you make while reading? How much of your own experience helped you figure out what this story is about?

Eric's Response: A huge problem I have when reading this book is flying through the text and not looking at the visuals. The text moves so fast, and i rarely remember to check out the accompanying visuals. Dawson has similar thoughts on this. I always think back to the picture books we used to read, and I think that over time our minds have been trained to look at the text, as opposed to the visuals. It is a matter of young minds and older minds. The challenge I am facing is to loose the mindset of textual thinking-only, and incorporate the visuals. I tried this out with the very short packet we read and it worked fine, but the second we get a bigger novel, I feel the need to rush to the finish.

Brielle's Response: While reading ABC I realized that I couldnt just accept what didnt make sense to me. It bothered me throughout the rest of my reading. My confusion started on page 198 when Jin Wang got a new face. Instead of just accepting it I tried to read deeper and understand what happened. What did his parents say when he changed? Did he run away? So after that I went back into Danny's story to try and find out how that situation worked . . . I know I probably was just reading too far into it. This is how I read though and I was (and still am) confused about how they delt with Jin Wang's transformation AND suddenly moving just because Jin Wang/Danny wanted to.

Asking students to point out what they believe to be the most important images almost always leads to rich discussion of form, as does focusing on their confusions. It is imperative to reinforce through classroom environment, assessment, and other activities that students' personal responses to literature are primary.

LOOKING AT THEME: PERCEPTION

I believe the most important aspect of Yang's *American Born Chinese* is the reflection it prompts in students about the way human beings perceive of themselves and the way this is connected to how they believe others perceive them. Jin Wang's struggle in the story over how others see him as the overly exaggerated Chinese stereotype, Chin-Kee, in contrast to Wei Chen's contentedness with his racial identity, is especially relevant for both younger and older teenagers. It is also an issue that many adults revisit throughout their lives as their roles change due to marriage, loss, parenting, and career changes. Human beings engage in reenvisioning themselves and reconstructing feelings and perceptions of themselves or others constantly. Students who observe the Monkey King's journey of transformation in parallel with Jin Wang's rejection of self are introduced to a common theme that is present in the works of classic literature and open to examination using the lens of psychoanalysis. In this respect, *American Born Chinese* is open to pairing with a plethora of other texts, topics for discussion, and subject areas.

LOOKING AT THE HOW AND WHY IN WRITING

American Born Chinese can certainly be used with younger learners to focus on reading comprehension or to identify basic literary or artistic techniques, but I find that with more mature students, I can use the text as a springboard to analyze the *how and why* of the text, which requires more sophisticated critical analysis and thesis statement development in analytical essay writing. The following writing prompts I use with students at the end of the three-text unit that includes *The Arrival*, "Two Kinds of People," and *American Born Chinese* propel students to think critically beyond basic identification of concepts or plot retelling in their writing, which most teachers would agree plagues student composition on the secondary level.

Sample Writing Prompts

> Analyze the theme of transformation in Yang's *American Born Chinese*. Who or what transforms and why? Please refer to various examples and details from the text to support your analysis. In your conclusion, comment on whether you think the way the author chose to convey the theme of transformation is effective.

Describe the influences on your understanding as you read *The Arrival*. Consider your presuppositions, assumptions, and experiences and how they informed your conclusions about the meaning of the story. You must provide concrete examples from your interpretation of the text in your response.

American Born Chinese is aimed at a middle school audience, but the exaggerated racial stereotype of Chin-Kee is often criticized as inappropriate and offensive. With this in mind, argue whether you believe Gene Luen Yang successfully executes his story about racial identity in *American Born Chinese* in a way that benefits young readers or merely reinforces a negative stereotype. Describe how the author is or is not successful by providing direct, specific examples from the text.

Choose Chapter 1 from *The Arrival*, "Two Kinds of People," or *American Born Chinese* and analyze the relationship between form and content. How do the various comics techniques implemented by the author and illustrator contribute to the development of the central theme in the story?

Some benefits to using shorter, more manageable graphic texts is that teachers and students can spend more time practicing ELA and twenty-first century skills, and less time slogging through difficult texts that fail to foster authentic and relevant dialogue or passionate writing. I can spend more time helping students develop reading and writing skills in the classroom, rather than assigning the traditional reading and essay writing for homework for which they are without guidance and more likely to look online for more authoritative interpretations.

CONCLUSION

My eleven-year-old daughter understood *American Born Chinese* on her own quite well, and based on our conversation about the book, she enjoyed it. But as this chapter shows, using graphic novels in a twenty-first century classroom can certainly increase students' enjoyment of the reading process *and* foster important literacy skills. I use *The Arrival*, "Two Kinds of People," and *American Born Chinese* at the beginning of the graphic novel course with seniors to teach them about how reading works and to develop their confidence for reading more challenging texts. The texts are tools for exposing developing readers to various strategies and dispositions of good readers, introducing basic literary concepts (such as multilayered plot structure, allusion, and characterization), connecting content and form, as well as gaining practice reading pictures as the language of graphic narrative. All three texts promote ample discussion of themes, as well as artistic and literary techniques fostering the social skills and behaviors necessary to perform in an academic community. All of these concepts and skills are easily applied to students' discussion of other texts and learning in other realms. Plus, kids enjoy the reading experience and do not associate it with work, making them more willing and open to other reading experiences. The job of the teacher then is to continue to help students feel successful, to promote positive attitudes toward reading, and to help them progress to more challenging texts to foster further skill development and knowledge acquisition.

Following Kenny's initial comments shared early in this chapter, he went on to report the following in his end-of-course portfolio reflection: "Graphic Novels have taught me to enjoy school books while I read them. The technique of slow reading to absorb not only the words but images has countered my past reading flaws." Thanks to a positive experience in the graphic novel classroom, there's one better reader in the world.

3 Looking at the Big Picture

Will Eisner's *A Contract With God* and *A Life Force*

"Do you believe in karma? What is justice? Why should we be good?"

These are some of the big picture questions I ask my students while they read Will Eisner's *A Contract With God* (2006a). Asking them to respond to the notion of justice and how they understand the universe and their place in it in a 5-minute quick-write in journals as a warm-up activity primes students for the deeper issues they are about to discover as they read, reread, discuss, and write further about both Will Eisner's *A Contract With God* and *A Life Force* (2006b). Looking at Eisner's seemingly simplistic drawings leads students to think critically about existential themes and to look at the big picture of their own lives.

TEACHABLE TOPICS, CONCEPTS, AND SKILLS

Table 3.1 Teachable Topics, Concepts, and Skills in Will Eisner's *A Contract With God* and *A Life Force*

Topics and Concepts	Skills
Religion and religious traditions	Active reading
Fate	Interpreting text and images
Justice	Rereading strategies

Topics and Concepts	Skills
Existentialism	Critical analysis of text and images
Human suffering	Making comparisons
Covenants and contracts	Writing practice: journal prewriting, reader response, essay of comparison
Loss	Oral discussion and listening
Six degrees of separation	Finding and using textual evidence to support a claim
Decision making	Making inferences
Cause and effect	Arriving at conclusions
Identity	Group collaboration
Violence	Metacognitive reflection
Economics	Applying concepts: empathy, stereotypes, storytelling, kinds of stories
The Great Depression (1930s New York)	Symbolic representation in writing and image
Survival and basic instincts	Analysis of aspects of story: setting, theme, plot, character, conflict
Nature versus nurture	Evaluating cause and effect
Neighborhoods	
Social conditioning; effects of environment	

A Contract With God is a collection of four graphic narratives about life on Eisner's famed Dropsie Avenue in the Bronx. In the story "A Contract With God," Frimme Hersh wrestles with the meaning of justice as he mourns the death of his nine-year-old daughter and questions his long-standing relationship with God.

Justice is also thematic in the stories "The Super" and "The Street Singer," where individuals struggle to get basic needs met and find relief from the demands of environmental forces. The final story, "Cookalein," conveys a coming-of-age story appropriate only for older high school students because of its sexual imagery. The influence of the environment on the individual characters in all four stories is prominent, overlapping in other interesting ways that lend to creative lesson development. Eisner's

From "A Contract With God" by Will Eisner, copyright © 1978, 1985, 1989, 1995, 1996 by Will Eisner, in *The Contract With God Trilogy: Life on Dropsie Avenue* by Will Eisner, copyright © 2006 by Will Eisner Studios. Reprinted by permission of W.W. Norton.

narrative structure of *A Life Force* reveals how one's destiny may not be the result of a higher power or fate at all but rather rests in the actions and choices of one's neighbor.

Looking at the Universal Human Condition

Eisner's stories prompt students to consider their place in the universe and the ways they understand it to work. If you are looking to explore essential questions related to the universal human condition and other existential themes in your classroom, Eisner's graphic novels are tools easily paired with literature that deals with fate, karma, justice, suffering, or religious and moral values. In addition to discussing the topics above, I ask my students to develop ideas about the purpose and importance of stories in people's lives and to define criteria for both effective storytelling and quality composition. In addition to their themes, Eisner's graphic novels are powerful tools for teaching students how to become better readers and writers because of the graphic novel format. I can ask my students to read each of the stories in *A Contract With God* for pleasure first and then reread for more thorough comprehension. Because graphic novels are composed of images, students report that they find themselves more willing to revisit them, something they are typically unwilling or less able to do using longer, print-based works. Students tell me they can remember particular portions of graphic novels easily and quickly, and because of the manageability of Eisner's shorter stories within *A Contract With God*, they feel more success reading. I also have seen my students' writing improve for their inclusion of detail and frequency of citing the text (a chronic problem in student composition) because the texts are more manageable and the images are more memorable. It is awesome to see a student locate an image in the text to revisit during class discussion and watch all the other students feverishly turning pages to find the reference. The sense of community that develops around looking at and discussing images is an essential part of students' pleasurable experience reading graphic novels.

Looking, Lingering, Learning

Since the graphic novel format lends itself to easier and more efficient rereading, it encourages closer "looking," where students might linger to contemplate images, fostering deeper comprehension, and leading to a more personal and intimate reading experience. While lingering, students have both time and space to consider their thoughts and feelings, and metacognitive reflection also can occur. With a teacher's direction, students can then learn to become aware of their prior knowledge and experience as it relates to making meaning.

In the lessons and examples in this chapter, you will see that revisiting the text and additional rereading is fostered by focused discussion activities of both content and form. Students are asked to reconsider initial conclusions drawn from first readings through collaboration and to develop an argument related to the relationship between words and images in Eisner's texts. They also discover how empathy is conjured through images alone and a combination of images and words in sequence. Students also compose comparative and argument essays, while also developing criteria for good writing and peer assessment using standards created collaboratively. Prewriting activities include reader response, journaling, and discussion, all of which show students that the reading process is as recursive and constructive as the writing process. Students also work on the organization and structure of the analytical essay, as well as developing thesis statements that reflect more sophisticated critical thinking. Overall, the student work in this chapter illustrates the value of using quality graphic novels in a classroom to foster ELA development.

"A CONTRACT WITH GOD"
READER RESPONSE

After the initial warm up activity, students read "A Contract With God," the first short story in the longer work of the same title. I ask students to complete reader response questions during the following class period, which forces them to revisit the text a second time. The prompts and responses can be used in any number of ways to foster discussion, debate, group work, or various forms of writing. The examples below show a few possible prompts and student responses.

Reader Response Prompts and Example Student Responses

> How does Eisner alter his lettering style to emphasize or dramatize emotions in the novel? Provide at least one example and note the page number.

Justina's Response: On page 4, Eisner alters the words, "All day the rain poured down on the Bronx without mercy." These words are drawn like dripping rain drops. These words add the emotion because they are dreary like the mood of the story.

> What image in the story did you respond to most strongly? How did you "read" this image? How did it make you feel? Why did you feel this way?

Alex's Response: The image on pg. 31 really stuck out for me.

From "A Contract With God" by Will Eisner, copyright © 1978, 1985, 1989, 1995, 1996 by Will Eisner, in *The Contract With God Trilogy: Life on Dropsie Avenue* by Will Eisner, copyright © 2006 by Will Eisner Studios. Reprinted by permission of W.W. Norton.

I know what this image on the next page is saying; it is simply demonstrating the drastic change Mr. Hersh had made in his life at this point in time. It was at this moment that he decided being moral

From "A Contract With God" by Will Eisner, copyright © 1978, 1985, 1989, 1995, 1996 by Will Eisner, in *The Contract With God Trilogy: Life on Dropsie Avenue* by Will Eisner, copyright © 2006 by Will Eisner Studios. Reprinted by permission of W.W. Norton.

wasn't worth it. This image was really hard for me to see. I feel like I've always been a pretty ethical kid. However, I've seen this in real life with kids in my grade. Kids decide that being cool is more important than their original values so they decide to abandon them and become a completely different person. Kids growing up and changing who they are is something that's always made me upset, and seeing this with Mr. Hersh evoked the same feelings.

> Describe the artwork. How does Eisner's particular style help to tell the story? Be as specific as you can in your response.

Dan's Response: Eisner's style is black and white that is somewhere in the middle of iconic and realistic. It helps to make the story feel more believable but also it gives the reader the ability some way to relate by not making the characters too detailed. Also, color is not used, I believe, because it takes the focus off of what the story is really about.

> What is the purpose of an epilogue? What does the inclusion of an epilogue mean in this story?

Ethan's Response: The epilogue is meant to show that this story never ends. The idea that somehow we can control and condense God's will ourselves is a never ending goal that we as a species will never cease to try and be able to do. Unfortunately, every attempt we have made has ended in the same manner and will unlikely change with future attempts.

> Describe how empathy works in "A Contract With God."

Gabby's Response: Empathy works in a Contract with God, because every person on this planet is worrying about the same thing and asking the same thing. Therefore everyone is really intrigued and engaged into this book because it effects there life on a personal level, they have no other option to express emotion, they basically can't help it because this novel has to do with real life!

Stephen's Response: Empathy is one of the only things that makes Frimme Hersh a bearable character in the second half of the story, since we have seen WHY he has fallen to such greed and thus feel bad for him rather than being overwhelmingly angry at him. It transforms him from a villain to a tragic hero.

More Ideas for Talking About Graphic Texts

In addition to the reader response journal questions above and to posting answers to the most important image in the text in our online discussion forum for homework below, students also discussed "A Contract With God" in class. The following general questions are applicable to most graphic narratives and others are specific to "A Contract With God." Several additional questions and prompts are located on the companion website (www.corwin.com/graphicnovelclassroom).

Generic Questions Applicable to Any Graphic Novel

- How did you feel when you saw ____ image or read ____ words on page ___?
- What did you think when you saw ____ image or read ____ words on page ___?
- What personal experience influenced how you felt or thought as you did?
- What specific aspect of the text caused you to feel or think as you did?
- If you formed a hypothesis about an image you saw, what assumptions and preconceptions is your hypothesis based upon?

Suggested Discussion Prompts for Will Eisner's "A Contract With God"

1. Examine the lettering in the text.

2. "Tears of angels" introduces sadness with words. How does Eisner create sadness without words?

3. Does Eisner use stereotypes in the story to convey meaning efficiently?

4. Where in the text do words match or not match the images?

5. As readers, we see Frimme both from inside the window and from the outside looking in at him on pages 13 and 14. Discuss the varied perspective and audience involvement in the meaning of how Frimme is perceived.

6. How does Eisner convey Frimme's emotion without showing him at all on page 24?

7. On page 25 are three individual images separated by space from top to bottom. How is God represented on this page? Is this the kind of page you pictured when you thought you'd be reading graphic novels?

8. How did you read the three panels on the bottom of page 28? What do those three pictures in sequence mean?

9. How does Eisner indicate that motion is happening or that time is passing on page 28?

10. How does Eisner indicate that time is passing using words in the text so far? (See pages 14, 16, 17, 29–31.)

11. Have you ever been angry about something that happened over which you had no control?

12. If you could add words to page 27, what would you add and why?

13. Does your perception and judgment of Frimme change when you compare the contrasting images of him on page 31? What do you see when you look at each image? Consider his body language/ positioning. Does that impact your interpretation? How much of *you* is in your interpretation?

14. Which techniques does Eisner employ to manipulate your reactions to the story?

15. Examine use of shadow on page 43 and perspective and the angle of elders under Frimme's looming presence. Who is vulnerable on the page?

16. On page 44, we cannot see Frimme's face, for it lacks detail and is blurry and the elders are a blur as well. Is this Eisner's way of making a generalization? Is he broadening this conflict to a universal experience?

Additional discussion prompts are located at the companion website.

Samples of Online Discussion

Teacher Prompt and Sample Student Responses

Choose one (1) image or panel you think best represents the main issue in "A Contract with God," the first short story we read in the larger graphic novel by the same title. Be sure to note the page and panel number, describe the image, then explain your choice. Also, clearly state and explain what influenced your choice. In addition to writing your own response, feel free to comment on others' responses.

Kailey's Response: "I think the most representative panel in the story was the first panel on page 27. I think that the main point of the story is that we can't control our destinies; no matter how hard we try to live by what we think is right, we still cannot create an outcome. If you are decieved into thinking that you can control these things than you will most likely be disapointed in the end. The picture shows Frimme with his hand up to the window, as if he has had enough with his "conversation" with god. By ending the coversation Frimme thinks he is in control of the situation, but in reality he has been talking to a window the whole time, so no one has been listening, and in my opinion he seems so foolish. I think my perspective and inerpretation of the story has stemmed from my atheist bieliefs, so I don't expect everyone to agree with me, it's just my opinion."

Abbey's Response: "I was intrigued by the words within the door frame on page 8. It gave the impression of the reader being inside the tenement, and the words being out in the rain. The blurb talks about how common it is to lose a child, and how anybody else would eventually accept it as a part of life. It introduces the dichotomy that once existed between Frimme and the rest of the world—everybody else was outside in the rain, but he was safe inside because he had a contract. Showing Frimme walking in the rain gives an automatic clue that now he's like everybody else. The contract is broken, and now the rain is falling on him as well."

The Primacy Debate: Pictures or Words?

Borrowing a lesson from my graduate school experience, I ask students to get into small groups to revisit the text and debate whether pictures or words are more important in conveying the story in "A Contract With God." In order to work on writing skills, I ask them to write an outline of their position on the whiteboard, including their reasons and supporting examples from the text. This lesson sparks heated debate and is a useful tool for emphasizing the use of evidence from the text to support a position both orally and in writing. The students collaborate to reexamine the text an additional time to formulate an organized response based on analysis. I then ask each group to assess the various arguments posted on the board in the classroom and evaluate the quality of reasons and examples provided in the outlines. Not only do most classes reach the conclusion that Eisner's pictures and words are inseparable in storytelling, they gain practice critically evaluating the quality of arguments presented. Students remain unconvinced of other groups' positions if not enough evidence is presented or when they discover illogical conclusions. Students are asked at the end of the unit to reapply these skills in a summative essay assignment located at the end of this chapter.

Looking at Comparison With "The Street Singer" and "The Super"

I ask students to read both "The Street Singer" and "The Super," allotting class time for sustained silent reading. After students read, I ask them to write a brief response and a list of items they would like to discuss during the next class, including questions, general comments, or problems found in the text. They are asked also to construct a rough comparison of the two stories as another prewriting activity for the summative assessment at the end of the unit.

Like "The Street Singer," "The Super" is a violent, tragic, and explicitly sexual story that conjures strong response from many students, providing an excellent opportunity for teachers to help students recognize the ways they read and the various influences on their reactions to literature. Dramatic irony and reader participation is also a substantial part of the stories' effectiveness in engaging students. My students form strong opinions about the characters, Rose, Mr. Scuggs, and even his dog, Hugo, in "The Super," and they are disgusted by Eddie's behavior in "The Street Singer," clearly showing their limited, teenage, twenty-first century perspective. With a little more understanding of life in the Bronx in the 1930s, students can revisit the text to carefully consider the issue of justice, survival, and desperation. Both "The Super" and "The Street Singer" prompt teenagers to consider the norms of sexuality and sexual behavior within the context of the story while examining their own standards of appropriate and inappropriate sexual behavior. This story also is incredibly valuable in terms of discussing identity and stereotypes and the often incorrect assumptions and initial judgments we make about others based on them.

Students often oversimplify judgment of characters as good or evil, but they learn from the sharply contrasting images in both "The Street Singer" and "The Super" how human beings are often a complex amalgamation of traits like depravity and compassion. The super is initially depicted as monstrous on page 98, yet the contrasting illustration of him mourning the loss of his dog on page 118 conjures sympathy from readers. I enlarge and project these images for students on the interactive whiteboard for close examination.

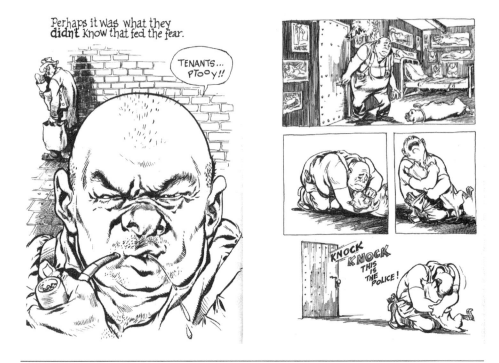

From "A Contract With God" by Will Eisner, copyright © 1978, 1985, 1989, 1995, 1996 by Will Eisner, in *The Contract With God Trilogy: Life on Dropsie Avenue* by Will Eisner, copyright © 2006 by Will Eisner Studios. Reprinted by permission of W.W. Norton.

Paying attention to their own reactions to these images teaches students that multilayered characters tell us much about how we view others and make judgments based on surface appearances and stereotypes.

"The Super" and "The Street Singer" provide excellent opportunities for students to pay close attention to their own biases and experiences as they interpret a text and for them to examine how they make judgments based on their interpretations of images. With guided instruction, students also can practice rereading to reexamine evidence on which they base their original conclusions and opinions. And through shared discussion of adult themes in Eisner's graphic novels, students gain maturity and experience handling sensitive and somewhat uncomfortable topics in an academic setting.

Writing Using Comparison

After extensive class discussion of "The Street Singer" and "The Super," students are assessed on their understanding of the stories by writing a multiple-paragraph essay comparing the two stories during a 55-minute class period. Another way I have students compare these two stories is to write a list of character, conflict, setting, and theme vertically on the whiteboard. I separate students into two large groups and each group collaborates to define the story elements for "The Super" or "The Street Singer" respectively, then we make comparisons as a whole class. Another way to do this is to draw a large Venn diagram on the board and ask each group to fill in their responses and discuss the results.

LOOKING AT *A LIFE FORCE*

Whereas *A Contract With God* contains four short stories, *A Life Force* is a great way to acclimate students to sustained reading of a longer and more intricately constructed graphic novel. Several separate story lines are interwoven in *A Life Force*, the structure directly related to the dominant theme of the interconnectedness of the lives of human beings, including its positive and negative effects. Eisner orchestrates the actions and events within a symbolic microcosm of the universe called 55 Dropsie Avenue. The residents' choices and behaviors affect the fate of the others, unbeknownst to them yet obvious to the reader. The dramatic irony draws readers into active participation with the story and begs the question of how much control any of us have over our lives. Eisner seems to suggest that events commonly attributed to God, universal design, or nature are instead caused by a chain reaction of human activity or mere coincidence. The central character, Jacob, finds himself in an existential crisis when he realizes he may no longer build as a carpenter, which gave his life purpose. He questions his reason for living and is troubled throughout the novel by the fact that his family cannot comfort him in his distress.

From *A Life Force* by Will Eisner, copyright © 1983, 1984, 1985, 1988, 1995 by Will Eisner, in *The Contract With God Trilogy: Life on Dropsie Avenue* by Will Eisner, copyright © 2006 by Will Eisner Studios. Reprinted by permission of W.W. Norton.

Jacob's situation prompts students to think about their own life's purpose, an especially relevant topic for seniors who are about to graduate from high school.

FRAMING *A LIFE FORCE*

Explaining or providing students with background information or creating activities that will help students understand basics about public companies, stock exchanges, and investors might be a good idea before or during reading *A Life Force*, as well as providing students with a basic historical context of the 1930s, the Great Depression, and communism. You also might encourage students to read the fine print in the various newspaper articles Eisner includes at the beginning of various chapters, since they relate to the economic and physical conditions of the period and are an important piece of the novel's setting. Each time I have taught *A Life Force*, students are completely confused by the thug who is accidently killed in the alleyway by Aaron. Eisner's artistic use of stereotypical thugs is visually confusing and sometimes frustrating for students, so you might give them an early warning about this. Other problems associated with reading *A Life Force* include its multiple characters and simultaneous plotlines. Students had trouble managing the relationships between the characters, so it is helpful to construct a visual map for students either before or during reading. A few other items students called "problems" with their reading included the chapter about Aaron, the shut-in who seemingly has no relationship to the rest of the novel. Most often, the problems in a text are the richest place for learning and may be the place you begin discussion with students.

A LIFE FORCE READER RESPONSE

The *A Life Force* journal prompts listed below illustrate how I prepare students to think critically about the definition of "good literature" about which they will write their end-of-the-unit essay. I ask students to make comparisons, this time a broader comparison of a novel and a short story as opposed to finding comparisons between two shorter stories within a novel as they had already done in *A Contract With God*. I also focus on helping students understand the difference between reasons and examples to eliminate this confusion often found in their writing. The questions also allow students to express their unique experience reading the novel and to draw final conclusions about Eisner's work.

A Life Force Character Map

Frieda Gold

Rifka Shtarkah ★

mother of

Daniel Shtarkah

mother of

Rebecca Shtarkah ★

married to

escapes Nazi Germany with the help of

has an affair with

father of

Jacob Shtarkah ★

father of

"The Black Hand"

work for

indebted to

is in love with

works with

helps

Elton Shaftsbury ★

Angelo Fiore ★

saves

Max

married to

brought to America illegally by

attack

Maria ★

Communist Revolutionaries

works for

supports

hates

Willie ★

father of

Morris ★

try

to

mug

coincidently saves

Moustache Pete and Lupo

interferes with mugging, Lupo is accidentally killed

Aaron ★

★ lives at 55 Dropsie Avenue

● 65

1. Describe how Eisner weaves multiple story lines together in *A Life Force*. What meaning does he intend for us, his audience, by structuring his graphic novel in this way?

2. Discuss the similarities and differences between *A Life Force* and "A Contract With God" (the first story in the larger novel by the same title).

   Which work did you like best? State your reasons clearly and refer to details from the texts to support those reasons.

3. Does Eisner's work qualify as "good" literature? Could you compare it with other novels or short stories you have read in school in the past?

4. Write a brief letter to Will Eisner about his graphic novels.

Asking Big Picture Questions

After reading and discussing *A Contract With God* and *A Life Force*, students work in groups to discuss the nature of literature before attempting to analyze how good literature is determined. Students conclude that Eisner's novels qualify, but I ask them to think about how they arrived at that judgment and to examine the criteria applied in making this determination. The discussion prepares them to write their final essay and to develop rubrics for their own writing. When students debated the criteria of good literature, it led to a consideration of the role stories play in our lives and in our culture. As Olivia's blog post below indicates, students can be quite adept at thinking through an essential question and forming important opinions about the nature of stories and what qualifies as good literature. Here, Olivia thinks for herself beyond our class discussion in her blog:

Last week in class we were talking about what makes good literature, and why so many high school students are so apt to describe *The Awakening* (for example) as "the worst book they've ever read." (Of course, I've heard the same thing about *Ishmael*, *A Separate Peace*, and *The Glass Castle*, so it's hardly a unique phenomenon.) And I realized, a short while afterwards, that the key to this debate is pinpointing the difference between what's *good* and what's *enjoyable*. I think we, as a society, have some kind of objective idea of what makes good literature and what makes bad literature—it varies from person to person, of course, but if you were to take a survey of everyone in the country you'd probably be able to compile a usable list. I'd never say *The Awakening* isn't good literature, because it's well-written and it tells a story that needed to be told at the time—but I'd also never read it again without being paid significant sums of money.

Enjoyable literature is a trickier label, because it varies depending on age group and background and plain old personal taste, and there's no agreed-upon definition like there (generally) is for good and bad literature. It's a source of constant fascination to me that I'm generally able to discern between great literature and enjoyable literature, and yet the two don't always overlap when it comes to my tastes. For example, I'm well aware of the problems with the Harry Potter series. I know its faults—I critique them often, in fact—and I'm certainly not one to say it's the greatest piece of literature *ever in the world* . . . and yet, when faced with a choice between reading Harry Potter or reading *Lord of the Flies*, I would choose the former, even though I know the latter is, in nearly all aspects, a better book. Does this mean that Harry Potter is a better book for me even though it may not be the better book when considered by society at large? Does anyone else have any thoughts on this?

Big picture questions play an important role in ELA instruction. Jim Burke (2010) discusses essential questions that prompt students to think for themselves and to think critically about literature as providing answers to such questions. Big questions ask students to get beyond plot-level detail and consider the more essential, philosophical questions related to humanity. At my high school, we use the core texts in our Grade 12 curriculum, which includes graphic novels, gothic and global literature, as well as poetry to answer the essential question, "What is human nature and how do we know?" You can assume throughout this book that the themes and issues examined in each of the texts listed in every chapter are connected in classroom discussions to the central, essential question above.

More Writing Practice

After setting the groundwork for students' summative essay assignment throughout the reading portion of the unit, writing activities include providing students with model comparative essays and working in class to develop well-structured introductory paragraphs and effective thesis statements. The essay prompts are listed below. As previously noted, part of our class writing process includes developing general criteria for grading student essays, which then becomes individualized according to each student's particular writing goals.

Comparison Essay

Compare one or more of Will Eisner's graphic narratives (*A Life Force* or *A Contract With God*) with *one other classic novel or short story* you have read here at Masconomet. Use the specific aspects of story (plot, theme, conflict, characterization, and setting) as your comparison criteria. I do not expect specific page numbers for the examples you cite in the classic text, but a well-composed essay *will* contain specific references to the images and text in Eisner's work.

Argument Using Comparison

To begin, determine specific criteria to judge good literature. For instance, does a good story contain vivid imagery and realistic characterization? Develop criteria of your own and use it to *argue* whether Will Eisner's novels qualify as good literature by comparing them to one other classic text you have read in high school. Prove your argument by referring to specific examples in the short stories contained in *A Contract With God* and in the novel *A Life Force* that support the criteria you chose.

Alternate Essay of Comparison

Identify the various similarities and differences in Will Eisner's *A Life Force* and *A Contract With God*. Make your comparison based on at least three of the following: theme, artistic style, tone, character, setting, plot, or literary techniques like the use of irony, symbolism, and motif.

I ask students to judge Eisner's novel according to the standards used to judge traditional literature rather than asking them to include the technical elements of the comics medium in their evaluation criteria. Though we discuss formal aspects of the texts and the effect of images within the unit, the writing analysis focuses primarily on its literary elements, since I teach Eisner's texts before reading Scott McCloud's *Understanding Comics* (1993).

CONCLUSION

I use Eisner's novels at the beginning of my graphic novel course to intro-duce students to the adult content of graphic novels, help them develop confidence reading, show the connection between reading and writing as process, and acclimate students to the essential questions we will explore throughout our course. My intention is that discussion of images and the literacy skills practiced will be strategically applied to more complicated and lengthy graphic novels later in the course. Often students begin my course relatively unaware of the ways they read, so Eisner's texts provide a good opportunity for students to think about *how* they read and the influences that inform their interpretations. Eisner's texts also provide students who have little experience reading graphic novels with familiar aspects of story while introducing a few problematic issues related to read-ing in the comics medium. The content of *A Life Force* and *A Contract With God* also prompt them to explore personally relevant issues about human nature within a format suited for easy and frequent reexamination, one that fosters feelings of success, which is especially important at the begin-ning of any new adventure. As Katie's blog comments below reveal, many students were enthralled with Eisner's work, and instead of looking at the clock and packing up their materials before the bell, I had to tell them to stop reading! She wrote:

> This week we started reading *A Contract with God*. We started reading it in class on Wednesday and I thought it was funny because Ms. Bakis had to tell us to leave when the period was over because everyone was so involved in the book.

Part II

Looking at Memoir in the Graphic Novel Classroom

From "The Veil" in *Persepolis: The Story of a Childhood* by Marjane Satrapi, translated by Mattias Ripa and Blake Ferris, translation copyright © 2003 by L'Association, Paris, France. Reprinted by permission of Pantheon Books, a division of Random House.

4 Pictures, Perception, and the Past

Marjane Satrapi's *Persepolis*

"Marjane and I have similar influences on our view of the world. Marjane, as a child, has access to various forms of media, has strict curriculum in school, and listens to her parents. All these things influence her worldview. On page twelve, panel six, Marjane reads about Karl Marx in a comic book. As she reads, she adopts many opinions on government similar to what the comic book teaches, thus influencing her overall opinion of her own government, much the way what I read shapes how I think about the world."

—Zach Zeniewski

The excerpt above from Zach's quiz response indicates the similarities he sees between himself and Marjane Satrapi, author of the graphic novel memoir, *Persepolis* (2004, 2005). I think Satrapi would be pleased with Zach's recognition that a teenage American boy has lots in common with an Iranian girl, more so than perhaps he initially would have guessed based on his limited experience and narrow exposure to images of Middle Eastern people and their culture.

By making personal connections with *Persepolis* in the classroom, students develop self-awareness about the various influences on the way they see the world and how they think about people and places outside their own limited experience. In other words, they become conscious of perception. Though my students are aware of some of the cultural differences, tragic events, and seemingly extreme political policies in Iran, the message Satrapi conveys through her own life story shows them that all Iranians are not represented by their government and religious leaders, nor should all Iranians be associated with the prevailing images of the country pervasive in Western media (Smiley, 2008). Satrapi's memoir about growing up in Iran during the Iranian Revolution and her experiences as a teenager living apart from her parents in Austria broadens teenagers' perspectives and changes their previously held assumptions about life in the Middle East and the people of Iran. My students find Satrapi's memoir particularly relevant for they read her memoir as that of a young person trying to figure out the world and all of its mysteries, and in that sense they are more like her than not. It is for these reasons and the discussion of critical media literacy the novel elicits that *Persepolis* is an extraordinarily valuable text to use in a twenty-first century secondary classroom.

Teachable Topics, Concepts, and Skills

Table 4.1   Teachable Topics, Concepts, and Skills in Majane Satrapi's *Persepolis*

Topics and Concepts	Skills
Perception	Reading, writing, speaking, viewing, listening
Prior knowledge and experience	Identifying literary and comics techniques
Cultural bias, racial stereotypes	Practicing online discussion
Influence of Media on shaping worldviews	Collaboration
Middle Eastern, Iranian culture and history	Metacognition
Coming of age	Citing textual proof in writing response
Personal and political independence	Developing paragraphing skills in writing
Nationalism	Implementing visual imagery into writing

(Continued)

(Continued)

Topics and Concepts	Skills
The individual's relationship to society	Composition
War, religion, and gender	Understanding audience and purpose in writing and viewing
Family relationships	Critical media literacy
Humor	Film response; analyzing the influence of media
Genre study: memoir	Writing memoir
Review aspects of narrative (plot, theme, setting, character, dialogue, conflict)	Constructing visual narrative (memoir)
Iconography	Using models to create original stories
Symbols	Applying new knowledge of literary and comics techniques
Use of color versus black and white in comics	Analyzing visual symbols and contrast (color)
Social conventions and norms	Critical reading and viewing
Subversion	Critical thinking
Identity and personal expression	Problem solving
Violence	Building social meaning

In this chapter, student analytical writing, blogging, online discussion, and class activities reveal the themes in *Persepolis* that are relevant to students' lives, including coming of age, independence, nationalism, war, gender issues, the individual's relationship to society, religion, and the intertwining of political and personal history. Students' new knowledge and understanding of the formal aspects of memoir and its application to their own memoir writing also is included in this chapter to illustrate how useful *Persepolis* is in teaching aspects of this genre. I worked with students to improve their descriptive writing by implementing visual detail and imagery into their own attempts at composition using model comparisons of *Persepolis* to standard print-only excerpts from Mary Karr's *The Liars' Club* (2005) and *Lit* (2009). As developing memoirists, students also reveal consciousness and consideration of audience while composing a story of a childhood experience rather than merely repeating a situation, conflict, or memorable event. Through their own attempts to implement the conventions of memoir, students discover the balancing act of fact and fiction in effective storytelling.

FRAMING THE NOVEL

It is a good idea to provide students with historical background in order to help students see how Satrapi's life story is both very personal and very political, as there are a variety of references to both ancient Persia and modern Iran that are crucial to understanding the novel. In addition to a PowerPoint presentation on the Iranian Revolution, I read a PBS historical timeline (PBS Newshour, 2010) with the students during class. I then show students the PBS *Frontline* video "A Death in Tehran" (Garnsey, 2009) before reading *Persepolis* for two reasons. First, I want students to see Iranian citizens and a slice of life in Iran. The video shows people walking through the streets of Tehran as if it were a busy day in any major U.S. city. Although the documentary includes the very graphic scene of a woman's death during the 2009 election demonstrations, most of the footage shows the victim's life as more typical according to our conventional norms, including photos of her with her boyfriend, travelling, or with her family at home. Also, pictures are scattered throughout the documentary, like the one of Neda blowing out her birthday candles, which helps to humanize her and other Iranians who were among the violent and tragic demonstrations. My students' exposure to life in the Middle East is limited predominantly to news stories about war and political power struggles with the West. Because of this limited exposure to life in Iran, I use this video presentation to practice and discuss the need for developing critical media literacy skills. I ask students to respond to the following questions and then we discuss their responses to explore their perceptions.

Critical Media Literacy Questions
for *Frontline*'s "A Death in Tehran"

- How did watching this film make you feel?
- What did the film prompt you to think about?
- Think about the producers of this film and its target audience. Who made this film and why?
- Which techniques are most powerful in this film and why?

- What are your perceptions of the Middle East?
- How did this film influence the way you perceive Middle Eastern people?

Using Supplementary Texts

In addition to framing the novel with historical and political information, it is also helpful to supply students with an outline of Marjane's family tree, namely her maternal great grandfather and grandfather, before reading because students often have many question about how Satrapi's family is related to Iran's ruling history. In addition to the resources mentioned above, after students finish reading the first book, *The Story of a Childhood,* I supplement students' reading with an article from the *New Yorker* titled "Letter from Tehran: Veiled Threat, What Do the Iranian Protests Mean for the Country's Women?" (2009). There are striking similarities in this article to what Marjane Satrapi reports in *Persepolis,* as well as the *Frontline* video. I read the article aloud during class, and students follow along reading, listening, and underlining parts that remind them of Satrapi's experiences. The journalist interviews two women who experienced violence during their daring forays into public protest in Iran during the summer after the fraudulent election of President Mahmoud Ahmadinejad. Further, the article explores the gradually increasing role women have played in the political process from the 1906 Constitutional Revolution to the Islamic Revolution of 1979 to the present. Students make connections between what they read in a book in English class to other real-world media sources.

READING RESPONSE

Once students begin reading *Persepolis,* I balance the number of interruptions to students' reading flow. I try to give only pertinent background information necessary to supply students with a good, enjoyable start to reading the novel without giving the plotline away or spoiling their own exploration of the text. I am not always successful, but I try to aim for the sweet spot (Gallagher, 2009). Depending on your students, you might use the reader response questions and prompts for *Persepolis* located at the companion website (www.corwin.com/graphic novelclassroom) to check reading and comprehension or to propel class discussion. The prompts are designed for guided reflection, focused on important ideas or panels, and I have used them successfully in small group activities, assigning one prompt per group to write about and discuss along with process logs, freewriting, and drawing. I also have used them for focused analytical writing responses, as reading check quizzes, or to work on development using details and citation practice. A number of sample prompts and questions are listed below.

- Explain how the personal and political are related in this story so far.
- Describe Marjane's relationship with God.
- How is the issue of gender an important part of this story?
- Would Marjane's experiences be drastically different if she were a boy?
- How are Marjane's reactions to events or people limited by her gender?

CLASS ACTIVITIES

Activities students complete during the *Persepolis* unit include group discussion activities, paragraph analysis and an in-class essay to assess their understanding of the second book. For the first book, in groups, students were given one prompt to discuss as a group only after they individually completed either a process log, freewrite, reading reminder questions, passage choices, or metacognitive process reflection prompts about their reading so far.

Student Example Responses

- **Curtis's Freewrite Response:**

  It is interesting to read about other cultures around the world. It also gave me a chance to see how some cultures view America. On page 12 they talk about how young Vietnamese men (the Viet-Kong) were killed by Americans. In the book I am starting to see how communism and the hate against capitalism is common feelings where the story is taking place. I am confused in the novel with the girl constantly talking to God about being a prophet then she starts to change her mind.

- **Excerpts from Connor's Reflection Prompts:**

  I wonder where she lived in Iran.

  I began to think of her when she's old.

  I like the idea of how innocent she is because she's a child.

  I know the feeling of not knowing why.

- **Excerpts from Antonio's Process Question Response:**

  At such a young age, why would she believe she's a prophet?

  Confusing words: avante garde, veiled.

  Words of particular importance: veil, prophet, God.

- **Excerpt from Robbie's Process Question Response:**

  I connected with the character because I've tried coming up with my own ways of thinking that contradicted my parents who have explained why they think the way they do.

- **Excerpt from Alex's Choose Images or Passages Response:**

  Page 14 panels 5, 6 anger me because of how the police attacked people trying to save those in the fire. Also page 15 panel 1 angers me how firemen arrived 40 minutes late. Also page 25 panel 8 I find humorous how the little girl tried to understand her grandfather's pain by staying in the bathtub for a long time.

Online Forum

Students discuss the novel online using a list of prompts to provoke discussion. Sample discussion topics are listed below with excerpted student responses.

Question: How Is Persepolis II *a coming-of-age story?*

Andrea's Response: Persepolis II is definitely a coming of age story because this is were she finds who she is in her failures and success in life. This is important for people to read and understand because she is a real life example of assimilating into new environments and trying to adapt to the new life but failing in her new life in Austria. By Marjane's failures in Austria from being to young and not understanding the world around her but facing her distress she was able to understand suffering and going home to Iran she is able to feel the comfort of her family. While adapting to the new Iran (96–97) she starts to change her life. Marjane meets Reza (122) and with Reza she learns a lot about herself and who she is. That she not only finds out what love actually is and how it ends but voicing her opinions (130, 142) that allows her to gain new opportunities by creating a theme park (144). But in her time she realizes what she has to do and leaves to become who she really is and not live in a cage like she felt she was in marriage (163/7).

By doing so she is growing into her age as a young adult to live a better life for herself and not others.

Question: What are some of the major conflicts Marjane is forced to deal with in Book II?

Connor's Response: I think Marjanes biggest conflict is the one against herself. She struggles again and again to find her identity and strives to be accepted by others. She does things that she regrets later sometimes just to fit in or just because she has nothing else to do. Does anyone think this book is similar to american born chinese?"

Question: Compare Persepolis *to another graphic novel you have read.*

Robbie's Response: Did anyone else read <u>Blankets</u> for a summer reading choice book? I thought that <u>Persepolis II </u>and <u>Blankets</u> are similar in many ways. They are both autobiographical memoirs, and mainly focus on the author's teen years. The characters are also very similar. Marjane and her family come form a conservative country, while Craig from <u>Blankets</u> comes from a conservative and religious family and community. Both are straightedge and then exposed to drugs during their teenage years, however Criag refuses to partake. Also characters are rebels who stand out from their surroundings. If you enjoyed <u>Persepolis II</u> and haven't yet read <u>Blankets</u>, I highly recommend it. It is another coming of age story but the plot is very different and interesting.

Assessment

After students had read more than 100 pages of *Persepolis: The Story of a Childhood*, I ask them to answer the following prompts to assess their comprehension of the text and their ability to write coherent, logical paragraphs.

Reading and Writing Quiz

Write one *well-constructed, well-developed paragraph in response to* each *of the writing prompts listed below.*

1. Based on what you have read so far, compare the various influences on young Marjane's developing worldview with the influences on your worldview. Cite pages and panels that show those influences.

Your response should be one well-written, detailed-packed paragraph structured according to the outline on the other side of this paper.

2. Describe how the issue of gender is thematic in the novel so far. The image on page 6, panel 1, shows the split between religious values and modernism. Find panels that show how gender is thematic as your supporting examples in this paragraph.

3. Show how Satrapi utilizes a specific technique of the graphic novel form/comics medium to convey her story. (Think about the concepts learned in *Understanding Comics*.) Give and explain your examples.

Justina's Response: In *Persepolis* written by Marjane Satrapi, she utilizes the technique that Scott McCloud refers to as iconic characterization. Satrapi has undetailed faces of characters. On page 95, the faces of all the girls are basically the same shape, size, and expression. . . . Since all the faces are undetailed, the room for emotion expands. . . . Another example is on page 5 panel 1. The conservative women are blocky triangles, while the freedom women are curvey. The small changes in body shape show a lot. They are icons for freedom versus religion. Marjane likes the reader to take as much as they can from the story, and that is accomplished because there is not a lot of details. She is more concerned with the theme and message rather than the structure of the faces. . . . Scott McCloud's idea of icon characterization was portrayed effectively in Marjane Satrapi's graphic novel, *Persepolis*.

Reading Test

Persepolis: The Story of a Return **In-Class Essay**

Persepolis: The Story of a Return is about Marjane's life as an Iranian teenager as she pursues an education in Austria. Much of Book II focuses on her relationships. She has lots of experiences with friends, both male (friends, lovers, and husband) and female (her landlords, roommates, girlfriends). Describe how these relationships influence her view of herself and her personal values. Give examples from the text to support your response.

Student responses to this Book II test show developing writing skills and critical reading analysis. They also reveal how my students began to empathize with Satrapi's memoir. As I have noted elsewhere in this book, developing writers tend to include examples and details from graphic novels to support their analyses more frequently than when quoting print-based novels. I observe that students are better at recalling images and finding them more efficiently in a graphic narrative compared to print-based texts. When asked, students confirm my observations.

LOOKING AT GENRE: MEMOIR

In the graphic novel classroom, we often talk about particular panels we respond to while reading and share our favorites. The picture of Marjane's mother defending her against the teacher who was concerned about Marjane's desire to be a prophet reminded me of the time my mother defended me (even when I was wrong) in fourth grade when I ran away from school because the principal wouldn't let me play with the boys in the schoolyard at recess. My mother obviously knew that running away from school at ten years old in the middle of the day was wrong, but she defended me when the nun came to retrieve me at my house. I share my own memoir essay with my students as a model of how memoirists turn a situation into a story (Gornick, 2001). My students not only find this story humorous and entertaining, but it prompts them to think about their own childhood memories and how they might use these situations and events from the past to create stories of their own. This conversation, prompted by a single reaction to a panel, allows us to discuss how much of *us* and our experiences influence how we read and interpret, whether text or images. I point out that the event was unusual because it was both funny and dangerous, but telling this story conveys a lot about me and my personality when I was young. The event was unusual, but the retelling and shaping of that event as "story" conveys defiance and my keen sense of justice. I use an example of my personal reading response to discuss and model for students how memoir is constructed.

Memoirists use such isolated memories as the basis of their life stories, molding, shaping and embellishing them with writing techniques to please an audience. This is where fiction and fact intersect, a topic of discussion we explore in class and practice in the memoir writing assignment at the end of the unit. We also apply this knowledge to our reading by discussing specific places in *Persepolis* where Satrapi may have left out information or where she might have embellished. In this lesson and in others, what I saw in *Persepolis* differed from what students saw, despite looking at the same images and panels, reaffirming for students that the reading process is highly personal and constructive.

Picturing the Past

When students talk about panels and their reading experiences in general, it usually leads to further discovery of formal aspects of genre. In class, Ryan said he found the reading "cryptic," that "it jumped around a lot," which led to a discussion about the way we remember the past in pieces. Little snippets or scenes are strung together in memoir, and so what he noticed as problematic in his reading turned out to be central to the way memoir works. Whether students express what they read as problematic, entertaining, or maybe even boring (they do love to complain), this is exactly where ELA instructors can facilitate learning about form and technique. Additional examples of working from students' questions and confusions about a text are apparent in other chapters in this book.

Piecing Pictures of the Past Together

In the first book of *Persepolis*, Satrapi describes herself as a child and major political events, including violence that erupted around her, like Black Friday, martyrs being carried through the streets, and schoolmates parents' dying. These images are most likely memorable to her because of their dramatic element. Though other important details might be lost, pieces of the past in the form of recalled images can form the center of a story that can be embellished with likely description and detail by an author. Mike shared an example of how most people remember things by referring to his memory of the tragedy of 911. When he was in kindergarten "playing or reading or something" and "someone came to the door and told us buildings in New York had been hit by planes," he said that he only remembered the basic image of the scene, but he couldn't recall the details of the person who conveyed the news; he couldn't remember what he was wearing or even really what he was doing. He just said "playing or reading or something" because those seemed like plausible things to have been doing at school since many other days that's what he remembers having done. This, I point out, is the stuff of memoir—of storytelling. Memory is faulty, and when an event gets retold, blanks need to be filled in and details need to be added in order to create a more complete story, akin to completing closure in comics as Scott McCloud (1993) defines it. The questions that follow are: Does this retelling and embellishing make the story any less true? If memoir has some elements of fiction in it, how can we trust we are being told the truth? The reader response–based discussion of *Persepolis* above illustrates how student-led discussion can lead to exploring genre, and these important discussions also inform students' composition.

WRITING MEMOIR

Students are given the opportunity to compose a memoir in writing and in comics form. As part of our writing process in class, I conduct mini-lessons during which I share excerpts of Mary Karr's memoirs, *The Liar's Club* (2005) and *Lit* (2009) as models for writing memoir. As students respond to Karr's storytelling, we discuss her skilled use of dialogue, imagery, metaphor, and diction to convey a story to show as opposed to merely retelling an event from the past (Gornick, 2001). Each of the excerpts from Karr's work I use in class contains dialogue with and without use of quotation marks. She also uses the dash in many sentences to imitate the sound of a conversation comparable to how graphic novelist use conventions of the comics medium to convey meaning. Her use of simple words and humor draws readers in to a very conversationlike experience, and Karr's voice is quickly established by her distinctive style. I ask students to draw an image conjured by Karr and to circle instances of various techniques where Karr appeals to sensory imagery. This lesson is also useful in discussing diction, including the use of vivid, active verbs in addition to adjectives to add color and visual appeal to writing.

Imagery in Words and Pictures

Comparing the imagery writers create with words with the imagery contained in graphic narrative is an opportunity to show students, especially reluctant readers, that good storytelling exists in multiple forms. In order for readers to connect to a person, place, event, or intangible ideas, a good writer uses his or her tools to paint pictures, and these details are the same details that exist in the graphic art within the panels of graphic texts. For many students who hate to read, showing them the similarities between graphic novels they enjoy and other traditional print-based texts is important in encouraging them to be open-minded about the range of stories available to them for pleasurable reading. Using the first chapter from *The Liars Club* piqued students' interest as they begged me to tell them what the rest of the memoir contained. Karr had them engaged in the first three pages and wanting to read more.

Applying Technique to Composition

In another lesson I borrowed from a colleague, students see, touch, taste, and smell pieces of candy to prompt descriptive writing using sensory imagery. They are asked to describe sound while listening to an audio clip and to read one more example of writing about smell. Finally, I ask students to describe a favorite place using all five senses and we spend time guessing the favorite place based on their written descriptions. The final assessment requires students to implement newly acquired knowledge of the genre and effective techniques discovered using models in composing their own memoirs. I have recently expanded the memoir writing assessment to include composition in comics form and other multimedia formats that include any combination of visuals and words. These options tap into multiple intelligences and give students the opportunity to use or try their skills at storytelling using pictures. See the example of a student-composed memoir using comics (Luke's visit to the swamp) found on pp. 85–86, an additional example at the end of Chapter 5, and one at the companion website.

SUPPLEMENTARY MEDIA

The great thing about graphic novels in the classroom is the plethora of resources related to the authors found online. Many graphic novelists are available to watch on the Internet on YouTube or at publisher's websites (see links at the companion website). Another benefit to teaching graphic novels is the film versions available to view with students. My students watch the film *Persepolis* (Satrapi & Paronnaud, 2007), which combines both books and is very well composed using similar artistic composition as the graphic novels. We watched the film in French using English subtitles because the students felt the film seemed too Westernized in English, altering their original experience reading the novels. After viewing the film, students listen to an audio interview with Marjane Satrapi, (Smiley, 2008) and look at pictures of her on the Internet projected on the Mimeo. It satisfies the students' curiosity about what she "really" looks like compared with her iconic rendition of herself. Juxtaposing realistic and iconic images of memoirists is a lesson you might use with students to discuss McCloud's notion about identification through icons from Chapter 2 of *Understanding Comics* (1993), and in fact, Sarah Glidden, author of *How to Understand Israel in 60 Days or Less* (2010) talks about how she purposely depicted herself as more androgynous to help a wider range of readers identify and empathize with her experiences (Pedler, 2010).

CONCLUSION

As we finish our unit, I ask students about why reading *Persepolis* is important to them. Their responses include knowing that they need to leave their own small town and see how other people live in other places.

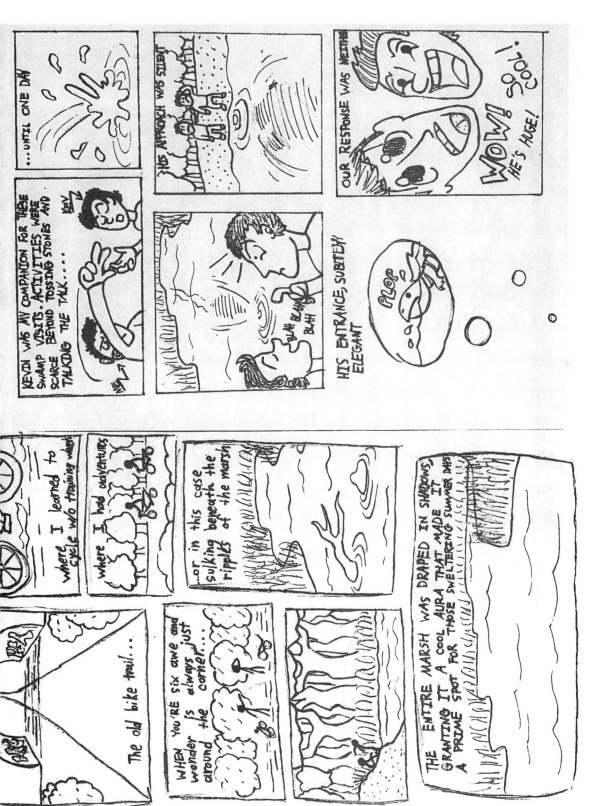

They report learning that people in the Middle East should not *all* be associated with images of terrorism as they initially believed at the beginning of our unit, and, like them, Iranians are human beings with families and friends, who face everyday problems just like they do. They also report learning more about human nature and integrity. *Persepolis* is a graphic novel popularly used in women's and cultural studies courses on the undergraduate and graduate level, but it is also an excellent text to use on the secondary level with teenagers who can relate to it as a coming-of-age story. My students relate to Marjane Satrapi as a teenager who is trying to figure out what she believes and how to stay true to the values her family taught her, just like they are trying to do as they get ready to leave high school. *Persepolis* is also incredibly valuable for its use in fostering critical media literacy. Not only should we try to use stories to educate, understand one another, and examine perception, we should teach students to be aware of the source of a constructed story and how its method of delivery can shape its meaning.

Allowing students the chance to shape their own stories of the past, those that are personal and important to them, enables them to understand the techniques of the genre and become more informed and critical readers. Composing them in multiple media formats also prepares them to express themselves using visuals, an important twenty-first century skill, while further appreciating the comics medium.

5 Leaving a Legacy Through Images

Art Spiegelman's *Maus*
Elie Wiesel's *Night*
Scott Russell Sanders's
"Under the Influence"

Ms. Bakis:	What are the unique qualities of a father-son relationship?
Eric:	Dads have to have "the talk" with their sons.
Dan:	They expect us to work hard.
Devin:	Dads teach their boys how to play sports or fix and build stuff.
Stephen:	There's competition. I like when I beat my dad at chess.
Mike:	Lots of stuff goes unsaid. Boys don't talk to their dads as much as girls talk to their mothers.
Ms. Bakis:	What are common problems between fathers and sons?
Connor:	Wanting to do my own thing that is different from what my dad expects.
Luke:	Boys have to be tough because that's what their dads expect.
Alex:	You don't want to make your father mad or disappoint him.
Antonio:	Competition!

The dialogue above is almost entirely recalled from my memory of classroom discussion a while back, and though perhaps somewhat inexact, it captures the gist of the responses I typically receive from male students at the beginning of our unit featuring Art Spiegelman's *Maus* (1986,

1991). Reconstructing the past from memory is as difficult as it is important, and in *Maus*, Spiegelman stretches the definition of memoir in interesting ways, raising the issue of reliability, accuracy, and the role of art in preserving history and personal legacies. His novels also force readers to reflect on difficult family dynamics, especially the unique relationship between father and son, and how the experiences of our past shape and color our present.

This chapter shows how students explore *Maus* and companion texts in my classroom, but Spiegelman's magnum opus offers many more wonderful topics for examination and is a useful text to explore in other subject areas, including art history and social studies. *Maus* has become a staple in Holocaust studies in many high school and college courses across the country. Because *Maus* is such a rich and complex graphic novel containing layers of meaning and metaphor, it is difficult to present all of the interesting themes and graphic-art-related discussions students conduct. I have done my best to include sample responses to activities, lists of student-created discussion topics, and sample personal letters to Spiegelman that hint at the plethora of critical analyses possible and empathetic responses among high school students in a language arts classroom. In addition to the lessons and examples I provide here, check the companion website (www.corwin.com/graphicnovelclassroom) for more help in creating your own unique unit.

TEACHABLE TOPICS, CONCEPTS, AND SKILLS

Table 5.1 Teachable Topics, Concepts, and Skills in Art Spiegelman's *Maus*, Elie Wiesel's *Night*, and Scott Russell Sanders's "Under the Influence"

Topics and Concepts	Skills
Conjuring images from memory	Group discussion and collaboration
Reliability and truth-telling in memoir	Critical analysis of text and oral discussion
Problematic nature of retelling narrative	Recalling textual detail from reading
Father and son, familial relationships	Making inferences
Role of art in preserving the past	Note taking
First person histories and genre study	Writing personal correspondence; considering audience in writing
Holocaust/ WWII	Composing memoir
Beast allegory, stereotypes, and identity	Implementing vivid imagery in composition

(Continued)

(Continued)

Topics and Concepts	Skills
Figurative language: metaphor, simile	Editing
Symbolism	Writing using active verbs to describe
What does it mean to be a witness?	Questioning a text
Family legacies	Identifying problems in a text
Time, distance, and representational art	Evaluating genre (memoir)
Generational themes	Activating prior knowledge and experience
How active verbs function in writing	Exercising empathy
Descriptive imagery in writing	Visual literacy

Like Elie Wiesel's *Night* (2006), *Maus* makes the Holocaust unforgettable. Spiegelman's retelling of his parents' experience surviving the death camps is an oscillation between past and present, where the author's guilt and self-doubt cast shadows over his attempt at an artistic rendition of both personal and global history in a medium best known for its cartoons. Spiegelman's dual struggle is conveyed using animals to categorize people (who at times escape neat categorization) and prompts critical analysis about memory and the struggle to use art to accurately preserve the past. Readers might understand *Maus* as a test of Art Spiegelman, both as the son of a Holocaust survivor and as a sequential artist.

Also a father-son survival story, Elie Wiesel wrote his memoir, *Night* (2006), to preserve the memory of the Holocaust and to "give meaning to [his] survival" (p. viii). I pair this text with *Maus* for its shared themes but also to explore the powerful role visual images play in how people remember things and in the art of composing stories about the past. Both Wiesel and Spiegelman make conscious attempts to use images to accurately retell an enormously important memory as part of their own history as well as the world's. Though incomparable to the degree of suffering of the Holocaust, Scott Russell Sanders is another son who grapples with his own identity as a survivor of an alcoholic father. In "Under the Influence" (1989), Sanders's ability to use language to craft vivid images serves as a useful model for developing writers. Like Spiegelman and Wiesel, Sanders grapples with guilt as it relates to his father and how one's past weighs so heavily on one's present. Sadly, because alcoholism is a relevant topic for many, students respond strongly to Sanders's essay.

After completing the readings in the *Maus* unit, I sometimes show my students the film, *The Boy in the Striped Pajamas* (Herman, 2008), which is also an excellent book (Boyne, 2006) suitable for middle school readers and beyond. I originally integrated the film into the unit because many students were curious about the untold stories of the SS soldiers and other people involved in the Holocaust. *The Boy in the Striped Pajamas,* though fictional, introduces curious students to an alternate perspective of the Holocaust and prompts further reading. *Anne Frank: The Anne Frank House Authorized Biography* by Sid Jacobson and Ernie Colon (2010), authors of the graphic novel version of *The 911 Report* (2006), is another Holocaust story in graphic novel format that might also interest students.

In addition to thematic overlap, using Spiegelman, Wiesel, and Sanders is particularly helpful in emphasizing similarities and differences in form. Wiesel and Sanders create beautiful imagery with words equal to Spiegelman's use of the comics medium, something I hope students appreciate through this intentional juxtaposition. Teaching graphic novels with a contemporary essay and a traditional print text is also meant to show young readers that great stories come in various packages.

FRAMING *MAUS*: DRAWING WITH WORDS AND PICTURES

After I ask students to define and share their personal understanding about father-son relationships as a warm-up for the unit, students commence reading "Under the Influence." After an initial reading for comprehension, I ask students to evaluate Sanders's writing style. The questions listed below attend to important aspects of language I hope for them to not only identify in this model but to implement into their own writing style. The response prompts also are used to activate prior knowledge and to help students examine the influence of a father on a son's self-image.

Scott Russell Sanders's "Under the Influence" Reader Response Prompts

- Even though the essay is about Scott Russell Sanders's father, what does this essay tell you about the writer, Scott Russell Sanders?
- How is this essay meaningful to you?
- Quote one example of a vivid scene Sanders "draws" with words.
- Quote examples of how Sanders uses sensory imagery in his writing. Give examples of each of the following: sight, smell, taste, touch, and sound.
- Describe the effect of the use of dialogue in this memoir.
- Draw a picture of one image Sanders creates with words.
- Create a comic (three panels minimum) of one scene in the memoir. Play with icons and symbols, and add text, including narration, dialogue, or both.
- Explain the meaning of the title.

I have used Sanders's essay many times in other units to teach various aspects of grammar, including parallel structure, active verb use, dialogue, and descriptive imagery. Brandon and Zach's illustrations below show scenes Sanders "draws" with words, emphasizing the useful connection between reading comics and teaching writing. (This is similar to what students do with Mary Karr's excerpt as part of the *Persepolis* unit in Chapter 4.)

Brandon's Response:

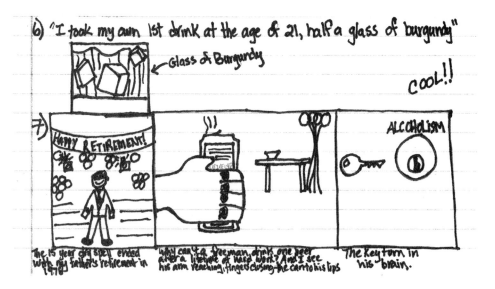

Zach's Response:

5. The dialogue is not the most important part of the story, nor is it meant to be. Rather it is meant to prove either his father's fear of looking disgraceful in front of his children, his mother's anger or Sanders' on desperation to ignore his father's slow decline.

6

Don't tell...

Mother slings accusations, he snarls back, she yells, he growls, their voices clashing. Before long, she retreats to their bedroom, sobbing — not from the blows of fist, for he never strikes her, but from the force of his words.

One particular impact of reading "Under the Influence" is the ensuing student response. Most of what teenagers report about drinking alcohol involves the physical danger and driving accidents, without as much attention paid to the effects it has on personal relationships and family dysfunction. Our classroom discussion includes a consideration of the pervasiveness of alcoholism in American culture and its effects on nondrinkers. The students also note the generational nature of this disease. Sanders addresses not only how his father's behavior influences the formation of his own personality and habits, but how this experience also affects how he parents his own children. Students' exploration of how an individual's choices and habits (or addictions) impact other family members in Sanders's essay foreshadows the nature of Artie and Vladek's relationship in *Maus*. As Sanders discusses what it means for him to be the son of an alcoholic, so too does Art Spiegelman convey the guilt and difficulty of being the son of a Holocaust survivor. Similar to Sanders's situation, the guilt that Vladek's survival imposes on Artie is a central theme in *Maus*.

LOOKING AT MEMORY AND IMAGES IN *NIGHT*

As additional prereading for *Maus*, students read Elie Wiesel's holocaust memoir, *Night* (2006). To frame this text, we listen to Wiesel's audio file reading of "A God Who Remembers" recorded on NPR's radio program, *This I Believe* (2008). Wiesel states, "Without memory, there is no culture. Without memory, there would be no civilization, no society, no future." Students are asked to respond to this quote and the essay in its entirety through writing and discussion.

Reading Response

While students read Elie Wiesel's *Night*, they record the most memorable images in the story in their journals. The following sample student responses show students' ability to visualize images while reading print-based text.

Dan's Response: The first part of *Night* I chose to write about is the scene that is described on page 17 with the Jews of Sighet being transported out of the ghetto and leaving their homes and personal belongings behind. The way Wiesel describes the scene really struck me, as he states, "it was like a page torn from a book, a historical novel perhaps, dealing with the captivity in Babylon or the Spanish Inquisition" (17). Being a Jew, I can picture in my mind the procession of people in the ghetto, sad and tired looks on their faces, as Jews marching into captivity once again. The historical reference allows me to picture this image and make a connection with what Wiesel is writing.

Devin's Response: On page 25, when the woman yells, "I see a fire! I see flames, huge flames!" This image is stuck in my mind. I can see the woman clearly and I can hear her yell out. It is a scary scene because I have been in a situation like that where I want to scream out like the lady. . . .

In addition to written response to reading *Night*, students also might draw the images they find compelling in the text.

In addition to the reader response activity above, I borrow writing prompts from First Person Singular, an excellent teaching guide found at the PBS.org website (PBS Teachers, 2002) to extend students' private reactions to reading *Night* and to further consider broader social and political issues prompted by the text. In a response to one of the lesson prompts, the real-world relevance of stories for students and the way personal experience influences reading and responding to them is illustrated in Josh's unfortunate real-world loss as he recounts being a witness to a fellow student's death in comics form.

In addition to using Elie Wiesel's *Night* to practice visualizing images while reading and other ELA skills, it also allows me the opportunity to provide background information about the Holocaust before teaching Art

Spiegelman's *Maus*. You can find Holocaust-related websites and links at the companion website to help plan your own unit.

LOOKING AT *MAUS*

Students bring their learning experiences of Sanders's and Wiesel's memoirs to bear on the themes and artistic style they discover in *Maus*. Before students begin to read *Maus*, I share a brief biography of Art Spiegelman and we listen to "Intersections: Of Maus and Spiegelman" a seven-minute audio presentation at NPR.org about the author and his book (Stamburg, 2004). In addition to links to historical Holocaust websites, I house several videos of Art Spiegelman and Elie Wiesel on our course website to supplement the unit as well. (These links also are listed at the companion website.) As students get to know Vladek while reading *Maus I: My Father Bleeds History*, I play sound bites from the tape recordings on NPR.org that Spiegelman used to interview his father while composing *Maus*. Students' hearing the actual voice of Vladek as he describes how Art's aunt, Tosha, his cousins, and his brother, Richieu perished adds an added sense of realism and power to the experience of reading *Maus*. (Perhaps the soon-to-be published *Meta Maus* DVD, which contains transcripts of Spiegelman's interviews with his father, also will be enormously useful in this regard.)

READER RESPONSE

I assign one chapter for students from *Maus I* to read each day and I quiz them on each. I use the quiz results as a way to hold students accountable for reading and as the basis of discussion of the text, which allows us to examine each chapter closely, together. As evident in the quizzes located at the companion website, plot-based questions are used to check reading completion where more interpretive prompts are meant to foster further analysis and discussion. I did not require students to answer all questions given on the quiz, so that during the review period our discussion would include clarification of textual details and competing interpretations. You might just as easily use the quiz questions as journal prompts or study guide questions for your students, or have them construct their own as they read.

Realism

As we work our way through assessing responses, students clarify their initial readings and add commentary about specific panels, passages, scenes, and events in the novel. The predominant commentary from students about *Maus I* is related to its realism. Students express an immediate and strong connection to Vladek as a real person rather than merely viewing him as a mouse, praising Spiegelman for his ability to conjure such response. Another personal connection with the characters in *Maus* is evident in my students' reactions to quiz question number twelve, where Artie reacts to his father's disposal of his coat quite passively. One student remarked that he would have taken his father's coat and thrown it away if his father did that to him, which swung our focus away from a discussion of Vladek's personality and why he would have thrown away his son's jacket to examining how Artie felt about the event and his response to his father's behavior. Students' recognition of the father-son relationship as part of the broader Holocaust survival theme shows how they interpret the multiple layers of meaning within *Maus*.

Spiegelman's Self-Doubt: Truth or Technique?

As part of our review of Chapter 6 quiz responses, the discussion centered on Spiegelman as author showing us, referring to, and questioning his own enterprise of composing *Maus*. This is the place in the text that Spiegelman questions his attempt to artistically reconstruct arguably one of the most sensitive and grandiose topics in history—the Holocaust. He critically evaluates and questions his use of the comics medium and other techniques, especially his choice of beast allegory. In this way, Spiegelman explicitly tells readers about his own concerns about being an artist trying to represent the truth and his fears of inadequacy of conveying the past accurately. Students and I discuss Spiegelman's method of showing himself as author within the very story he is composing (sometimes referred to as *breaking the fourth wall*) and whether this makes him more or less credible. It also causes us to wonder about defining *Maus* as strictly memoir. Artie essentially lies to Vladek on page 23 about promising not to include Vladek's story about Lucia, which is another example in the text where students and teacher might discuss Spiegelman's technique and memoir's inherent issues surrounding truth. Does the lie Artie tells make him more or less believable as author? The responses are usually split among students, some believing that everyone lies, which makes Artie seem more human, more credible, while other students believe he is being manipulative and therefore they are skeptical readers. Similar instances like this one are scattered throughout *Maus*, which creates interesting dialogue among students.

Because of such conversations that begin with quiz questions, students become far more aware of and interested in the complexity of *Maus I*. This type of close-reading experience and engagement in *Maus I* fosters more active and close analysis of students' reading and discussion of *Maus II*.

LOOKING AT TECHNIQUE

Students have ample opportunity when reading *Maus* to apply previously acquired knowledge of the formal aspect of comics to evaluate and think critically about Spiegelman's use of iconic mice and other creative use of symbolic icons, images, and panels. Spiegelman uses the image of the swastika in several panels and in various ways throughout both novels. The swastika on page 125 of *Maus I* is an example of how the image adds an ominous feel to Vladek's recollections that he and Anja "didn't have where to go." You also might tap into students' prior knowledge about the expressionistic nature of lines learned in Scott McCloud's *Understanding Comics* (1993) to discuss the intensity of Artie's emotional and mental breakdown over his mother's death in the Prisoner from Hell Planet excerpt on pages 100 to 103 of *Maus I*.

MAUS II LESSON ACTIVITIES

I give students the option to work in a group to read and discuss *Maus II* or to read independently and write their own response notes to later share with the class during our whole-class discussion of the text. Either way, students use technology tools to both discuss and submit their responses to me to preview before the assigned discussion day. Some groups form smaller social networks on our course website to blog and to talk using the discussion forum tool. Other students meet face to face, some used Google Docs, whereas other exchange e-mail. Students submit their notes to me prior to our whole-class discussion so that I can assess them for completion and eliminate redundant topics for our discussion. On discussion day, students are able to share their small group's discussion of topics in *Maus II* without repeating topics. The lesson instructions for students can be found at the companion website, and I have included sample student discussion topics of *Maus II* here.

Maus II Student-Generated Group Discussion Topics

- Why the masks in Chapter 2?
- The father/son dynamic: Do you think Artie is a good son?
- Obligation versus love; loyalty; how to cope in a difficult relationship.
- Why did Mala come back?
- Why is Vladek racist in the scene where he calls the black man a "shvarster"?
- What are the parallels between Artie and Vladek? How are they alike?

- The image on 116 of Vladek looming through four panels with photos at his feet is deeply moving.
- Vladek is made "historical" by his son or lives on in *Maus.* Is it irony that all he had left in his life were pictures and a story? Isn't that the graphic novel form?
- The gravestones at the end are sad, don't you think?
- Do you think Book II is better than Book I?
- What's up with Vladek and not remembering the orchestra? Isn't that a sign of an unreliable narrator? Did he just *refuse* to remember that part?
- How do we understand what another person sees or experiences? Does looking at art and story help us with this?
- Why should it matter how good representation is if it can't convey the actual reality itself? Why bother?

The comments below are excerpted from Brie's reader response notes about *Maus II: And Here My Troubles Began.*

On page 24 . . . The fact that you can still see the flies as they are interviewing [Art Spiegelman] can be paralleled to two things.

1) The Interviewers are metaphorically like the flies, constantly buzzing around him and pestering him, nothing more than a constant annoyance.

2) The bodies shown below him in the first panel are still there, and the reporters are stepping on them carelessly. While he's trying to get out a story about the holocaust, there are all these people either overanalyzing it or trying to exploit it. While people keep saying that everyone from these terrifying events should get their stories out to show the public the horrors of them, the public doesn't want the stories so they can try to relate to the disaster. They just want to be entertained by an interesting story. Reading the survivor tales won't change them. It didn't change me, because even though I read it, I wasn't THERE, I didn't die because of it. I can't empathize with it.

    Another thing I noticed in chapter two is Vladek's surprising amount of usefulness. It seems almost unrealistic, at least to the degree it was described. From his work as a tin man to repairing shoes, everything of which he seemed to do better than anyone else at and without any issues from the Kaposi or Generals. I guess that's kind of mixed with the issues of memory though. With Vladek telling the story of what happened and it being so long ago, there's bound to be things that he doesn't remember exactly as it happened, but his brain fills it in with events that seem more interesting or seem like they fit. It's impossible to remember everything exactly as it happened. Especially when you write something with dialog, there's no way to remember everything that everyone said.

Brie's comments and the list of topics derived from other students' collaborative questioning of *Maus* show the kind of critical thinking Spiegelman's graphic novels elicit from high school students.

LETTERS TO THE AUTHOR

Writing letters to authors is a fairly common assessment tool in language arts for its value in helping students flesh out their personal experiences reading and to think critically through writing about a text and its author. I ask my students to write personal letters to Art Spiegelman to gain experience writing for a real audience. Rather than mailing my students' letters to the author, I met Mr. Spiegelman at the 2009 American Library Association Annual Conference in Washington, D.C., and handed them to him in person (I received an autograph in return!). The following excerpts from students' letters and those located at the companion website indicate not only praise for Spiegelman but for the power of storytelling in the comics medium and its personal relevance for students.

For this particular assignment, students are assessed on meeting the content-related expectations of the letter as well as on the formal use of language appropriate for personal correspondence. We discuss the social ramifications and negative judgment of poor writing skills and plain old sloppiness through viewing sample e-mails that can be easily located online by Googling "poorly written e-mails." The students are advised that they will lose one point for every misspelling, typo, or other surface errors. I usually choose one or two writing assignments per year to hyper-focus students' attention to presentation and careful editing. For some students, the number of errors they realize they have committed startles them into becoming more vigilant about the "picky stuff" of writing. It can be a difficult lesson to learn, though one they don't soon forget.

Letter to Art Spiegelman: Student Excerpts

From Matt's letter: Well I am betting on the fact that the rest of the letters you get from my class will contain angry messages about your comic, *Prisoner on the Hell Planet*. Well I disagree with them. I would like to express my support to you on that matter, and in fact it was one of my favorite parts of your books. It was really emotional and I was able to empathize with it, I'm not sure why, I have not been in that situation but I could really feel for you. . . . Also, living in the shadow of your father's experience with the Holocaust was something I could relate to. Well my experience was nowhere near the level of extremity. When I was growing up my sister was diagnosed with a chronic illness and I always felt like my concerns or issues were less important, therefore I didn't want to bother my family with them. I bottled them up until one day I recognized how unhappy it made me and I came to the realization that what I was perceiving was wrong, and both our problems, mine and my sister's had the same value. I wonder if you have come to grips with the fact that a problem is a problem and every life has value.

From Dan's letter: Being Jewish, I have had images of the Holocaust thrown at me since I was a kid, and I was surprised by how your pictures still evoked the same emotions from me as if I were looking at an actual photo of the concentration camps. On pages 70 and 71 of Book II it seemed as if I was looking into the actual gas chambers at Auschwitz, and I broke down in tears when reading these pages. The horrors of the Holocaust have such a different meaning for me, being Jewish, and it seemed so real in *Maus*.

From Luke's letter: Let's get the bootlicking out of the way early on by saying that I thoroughly enjoyed your two volumes of *Maus* and was deeply moved by the work in what it was able to achieve in its presentation and medium. As an aspiring graphic novelist myself, it did much to cement my decision to live a life of creative toil and likely poverty. . . . Is there anything in the novel that you look back on now with regret for including? What about its unexpected success? . . . have reactions varied depending on the culture of the reader? Going into *Maus* I expected a visualized version of *Night*. Boy was I wrong. The way you made a story out of your efforts to craft a story out of your father's life was brilliant and caught me totally off guard. The effortless transitions that occur regularly between the 30s/40s and 80s were never disorienting yet lacked any sort of true pattern or marker. This was one of the most impressive features of the story, and I have yet to figure out exactly how you pulled it off so well. More so, it helped distance your father's story from the countless other Holocaust tales out there. It made Vladek feel so real, for better or worse.

Other Ideas for Writing about *Maus*

The possibilities for talking and writing about *Maus* are numerous. Students might use a variety of critical lenses to examine the text, including formal literary, psychoanalytical, historical, or artistic analysis. Student also might use *Maus* to learn how to write a research paper or to complete a multitext comparative essay. Drawing or writing a memoir using allegory is something I have considered, as well as asking students to begin with a problem they find in *Maus* and proposing possibilities for resolving it. Other ideas include exploring the problem of pain or human suffering, man's inhumanity to man, or the problematic nature of memory. I also have considered asking students to record an interview with their parents who might tell them a story about the past from memory, and ask students to retell that story in a medium of their choice. Additionally, students would reflect on this experience of second-hand storytelling and the inherent effects of the medium on their ability to be accurate.

In addition to these ideas for writing and the unit I implement with my students outlined in this chapter, many resources are available online to help you think about ways to use *Maus* in your classroom, which I have listed at the companion website. An interesting resource called *MetaMaus* tells the story of Spiegelman's process of creating *Maus,* including his authorial decisions and more information about Vladek Spiegelman, and it is due out in the fall of 2011 by Pantheon. A DVD is included with the book (which is not a graphic novel) and also may prove invaluable for informing your teaching of *Maus.* Spiegelman's graphic novels are so rich in both content and form, my example unit merely scratches the surface of what can be done using this text.

Conclusion

Students' commentary reveals their consideration of the challenges of the accuracy of memory and their evaluation of the quality of Spiegelman's representation (through art) of both personal and public events from the past. Students reveal their personal response and analysis of Spiegelman's efforts to artistically recast the truth and his ability to conjure empathy in readers. Students also examine expressionism through analysis of Spiegelman's use of lines and evaluate the author's expansion beyond boundaries of formal conventions of genre. Application of comics concepts learned from Eisner (2008) and McCloud (1993), as well as experience reading memoirs, is evident in Dan's graphic memoir of his earliest memory with his father.

Part III

Looking at Superheroes in the Graphic Novel Classroom

From *Batman: The Dark Knight Returns* by Frank Miller, trademarked and copyright © 2002 by DC Comics. All Rights Reserved.

6 A Glimpse of the Superhero Genre

Frank Miller's *Batman: The Dark Knight Returns*

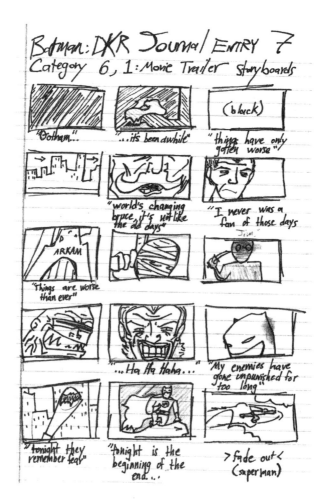

Luke's movie trailer storyboard shows one way students respond playfully and artistically to their experience reading Frank Miller's *Batman: The Dark Knight Returns* (2002), the graphic novel I offer to students as a glimpse into the best of the graphic novel superhero genre. Because of the recent slew of Batman films, most students immediately connect to this curriculum and are highly motivated to read; however, students often are stunned as well when they realize some of the difficulties involved in reading such an intertextual and complex graphic novel.

Students' reactions to reading *The Dark Knight Returns*, apparent in many of their responses to activities in our reading workshop that follow in this chapter, show tremendous critical and creative thinking as they grapple with a challenging text. But their responses also indicate students' relative inexperience with the superhero genre. What I love most about teaching this novel is that while students are deeply engaged in enjoying plot, vivid characterization and graphics, I can attend to the business of designing activities that exercise English language arts and twenty-first century skills.

In Miller's *Batman: The Dark Knight Returns,* an aging Batman returns from his previous decision to retire after the death of his sidekick, Jason, the second Robin, to face various sources of corruption in a dystopian Gotham City. Not only does Miller's Dark Knight grapple with a mutant gang leader who has risen to power in his absence, he also must face conventional foes such as Harvey Dent and the Joker while suffering from internal turmoil throughout the novel.

Functioning as a classical literary device, the news reporters and other media talk show pundits comment on the action of the ongoing criminal activity in Gotham and on the actions of the Batman.

From *Batman: The Dark Knight Returns* by Frank Miller, trademarked and copyright © 2002 by DC Comics. All Rights Reserved.

Examining the media's role in the novel and the panels in which they appear provides excellent opportunity to examine the influence of media on contemporary popular culture and the way people form opinions.

TEACHABLE TOPICS, CONCEPTS, AND SKILLS

Table 6.1 Teachable Topics, Concepts, and Skills in Frank Miller's *Batman: The Dark Knight Returns*

Topics and Concepts	Skills
Hero and superhero narratives	Independent reading
Role of media in culture	Metacognitive reflection
Government	Sustaining tolerance for failure, uncertainty, and ambiguity through difficult text (Blau, 2003)
Vigilantism	Willingness to sustain closure and take risks (Blau, 2003)
Subversion	Capacity for sustained, focused attention (Blau, 2003)
Plot and subplot	Critical analysis of text (film and comics)
Symbolism	Writing: focus on paragraphing and organization
Juxtaposition of images and plotlines	Writing using collaborative Web 2.0 tools
Flashbacks and backstory	Assessment (peer and self)
Characterization	Making comparisons
Understanding the logical progression of ideas	Discussion (online, in person)
Interpreting color and contrast	Collaboration
Intertextuality	Information and computer technology
Allusion (comics, cultural, literary)	Listening
Internal and external conflict	Critical and analytical thinking

Miller's graphic novel is appropriate for older high school students for its social and political themes, including justice and vigilantism. Batman's decisions challenge students to think critically about their own personal choices. Through examining traditional and changing definitions of heroes and superheroes, students can explore our cultural affinity for hero narratives. In addition to content-based considerations, I use Miller's text primarily to practice reading difficult text independently, further developing the traits of good readers (Blau, 2003) and to develop analytical writing skills. I know that several teachers at the undergraduate level focus heavily on intertextuality of *The Dark Knight Returns*, but it is challenging to focus too closely on Miller's impact on the superhero genre or on a deconstruction of its intertextuality with secondary school students since this is many students' first foray into reading superhero graphic novels. I help my students handle the various references to other superhero comics and the political history with which Miller plays only to clarify initial confusions and to aid their basic comprehension of the story. More sophisticated critical analysis will come with experience.

FRAMING THE TEXT

Before reading, I ask students' about their preconceived notions about heroes and superheroes. I have students write their initial definitions of heroes in their journals, and we discuss these definitions. Next, we discuss the relationship between human nature (our English department's 12th grade curriculum guiding question is: What is human nature, and how do we know?) and our affinity for heroes. I ask students to again respond in writing about heroes in the middle and end of the *Batman* unit to see if their initial impression of heroes has evolved. We conduct the same routine for superheroes to collect as many defining characteristics of superheroes as possible. In this unit and the next, which focuses on Alan Moore's *V for Vendetta* (Moore & Lloyd, 1988), students will question whether the Dark Knight and V qualify as superheroes according to the criteria they have constructed, in some cases through writing essays about their conclusions or creating their own superhero narratives.

It is imperative to provide students with background about superheroes and conventions of the genre to help contextualize their reading of *The Dark Knight Returns* and to make them aware of the references to other aspects of popular superhero narratives. One great way to do this is to show students the documentary, *Comic Book Superheroes Unmasked,* directed by Steve Kroopnick (2003), portions of which can be viewed on YouTube .com. Another good documentary resource is *Comic Books Unbound* (2008), produced by Stan Lee and Ron Pearlman. It shows the connection between comic books and the comic book industry and the Hollywood superhero films students currently see today. I also have students read the transcript of an NPR interview (Seabrook, 2004) with Danny Fingeroth about his book, *Superman on the Couch: What Superheroes Really Tell Us About Ourselves and*

Our Society (2004). The discussion questions for this reading assignment are located on the companion website (www.corwin.com/graphicnovel classroom). Your local comic book shop owner also may offer some expertise, as they are always eager to talk about comics with teenagers. I rely on the help of a colleague with whom I teach *The Dark Knight Returns,* and I bet you have a Batman expert somewhere in your school too. Having other adults share their enthusiasm and knowledge about superheroes adds further affirmation for students that comics aren't just for kids. You certainly should not feel intimidated about teaching superhero graphic novels because you may not feel knowledgeable enough. I was far from an expert when I began.

Don't forget to query your students about their familiarity with Batman to avoid unwarranted assumptions about your students' experience reading superhero comics. The vast majority of my students knew nothing about the character beyond his identity as a superhero, his costume, and his characterization in the most recent film, *The Dark Knight* (Nolan, 2008). The students who are experienced Batman readers will read and interpret Miller's *Batman: The Dark Knight Returns* very differently than the inexperienced readers, so encouraging these avid readers to share their insight can be a helpful classroom resource.

To provide a basic history of the comic book character in order to distinguish him from the most recent film character, I use an excerpt from the *St. James Encyclopedia of Popular Culture* (Wright, 2000) to provide students with a basic overview of Batman. This entry explains the origination of the comics character, including a history of the ways in which Batman has been marketed in film and television up through the appearance of Frank Miller's "darker" rendition, which has recently revived Batman's popularity. Students who conducted their research projects on Frank Miller earlier in the graphic novel course also shared information they learned about the author and his works with their classmates.

READING RESPONSE WORKSHOP

Batman: The Dark Knight Returns is a combination of the four-issue comic book limited series, labeled Books I to IV, so I divide reading response workshop activities accordingly for students to complete for homework and during sustained silent reading in class. I like to use the term *workshop* for activities that engage students in constructive, process-oriented reading, writing, and thinking, although literacy educators often use the term for more specifically defined pedagogy. The activities, some of which are listed at the companion website, provide ample choice for reading response and are commonly used in ELA classrooms with all types of literature to promote a variety of strategies for comprehension. I require my students to complete at least eight different activities, two to be completed as they determine while reading each book. The assessment does not intrude on their first reading, holds students accountable for independently reading the novel, and encourages active critical and analytical thinking through writing and drawing. In addition to Luke's visual response to reading *The Dark Knight Returns* that begins this chapter, additional examples of student response follow below.

Example Student Reader Responses

Lydia's reading responses show how she reflects on the way she reads, illustrating the mental participation graphic novels demand.

> Reading a graphic novel is very different from reading the kind of books I am used to. When I read a book that doesn't have any pictures in it, it is very easy to read; I don't have to think about it at all. Reading graphic novels takes a lot of thought from me. In Batman: The Dark Knight Returns, there is a lot of text as well as many pictures. I have to make sure that I remember to look at the pictures when I read. Although I feel that the pictures are not as important in Batman as they were in V for Vendetta or Will Eisner's books, they are still there for a reason, so I need to pay attention to them. When reading I sometimes have trouble understanding the layout of all the panels. There are times when I don't know which text to read first. It took me a few pages to get used to the news text being above the TV. I still have trouble with the gray narration boxes, I'm pretty sure they all represent Batman's thoughts, but sometimes they don't make sense.

The following response about how the main character differs from the reader shows Lydia's personal connection to reading and her understanding of characterization.

> I find Batman to be a very interesting and inspiring character. He represents the action no one takes even if they know something is wrong. In this way, Batman and I are different. Like Batman, I see a lot of things in the world that I don't agree with, things that should be stopped. Although I didn't start it, it's as equally my fault as it is the initiator's because I have done absolutely nothing to prevent or stop it once it's started. . . . We are different because Batman has the persistence to get what he wants and the willpower to make it happen.

The following response is about an image that raises Lydia's curiosity. Noticing Lana's lie is an important detail in assessing the role and influence of media on how we interpret events and judge people's behavior.

> Page 140, panel 8. Lana says that "Batman hasn't killed anybody" which is a lie. Although I, like Lana, am on Batman's side, I know that statement is false. He has killed so many people, but they are all criminals, so sometimes it isn't noticed as a bad killing, even though he still kills.

The following is from a freewrite that shows how Lydia understands Batman's internal conflict by making a comparison to her own self-understanding:

> I'm not sure if I really like <u>Batman</u> or not. Usually, when I read books for English, I either love it or hate it (most of the time I hate it!). With <u>Batman</u>, I can't decide. The character of Batman annoys the crap out of me. I wish he would just decide which side he was on, Bruce or Batman. I get that he wants justice and everything, but keeping Gotham safe from all the criminals isn't Bruce Wayne's job. When Batman was born, it became his job. You can't just quit or retire from a job that you elected yourself to do. For me, I wanted to learn how to play music. Once I got really good at it, I couldn't just stop, I still can't. Even if I stop playing, I still have music in me all the time. Once a musician, always a musician. This is why Bruce can't quit Batman. Batman is inside of him. If he walks around Gotham, he will see things not only as Bruce Wayne, but as Batman too. Batman is like V, an idea coursing through an individual and his soul, bursting through the seams until other people notice it.

The following response shows Luke's interpretation of the media as functioning as a character in *The Dark Knight Returns*. The reading workshop prompt asks readers to choose three words that describe a character and reasons for their choices.

> Character: The Media of Gotham City (Channel 2 News)
>
> 1. Desensitized: the news team of Channel 2 is willing to put anything on the TV, from taped murders to death threats from notorious gangs. They never appear squeamish, but excited to have something disgusting to show viewers.
>
> 2. Ignorant: When discussing issues, any argument is often overwhelmingly one-sided and when there is an opposing view it's

often heavily ridiculed and looked down on. Reports are often interrupted for an "expert" opinion that's either obvious or useless. Opinions rarely change and scapegoats are far too common. Criticism is never correctly directed and usually completely wrong.

3. Intrusive: No matter how personal an issue may be, Channel 2 needs to get the scoop, even if the scoop is slanted. They pick and prod at everyone, criminals, victims, "professionals", anyone who will talk. Unfortunately, their determination usually sticks them with assholes who want their opinions publicized. They never seem to be able to nail down decent people as witnesses, only bias or predjustice jerks.

These responses show students questioning the text, persisting through its ambiguity, thinking critically, and reflecting on the process of reading.

QUESTIONS TO PROMOTE FURTHER THINKING, DISCUSSION, AND WRITING

The reading response workshop activities serve as a precursor to class discussion of *Batman: The Dark Knight Returns* in which students share their various questions and reactions to the text. You might think about having brief discussions after each of the four books, half way through the novel, or one at the end of students' reading, depending on your students and other constraints or demands. I allow students time at the beginning of each class to share their responses or pose questions as they are reading throughout the unit. I ask students the more summative questions listed below to consider the text as a whole and aid a shared understanding of the novel. The questions are also useful for helping students to begin thinking about a topic they might like to examine in closer detail in writing. The questions below also might be useful to use for small group discussion or as quiz or test questions.

- Describe your experience reading Frank Miller's *Batman: The Dark Knight Returns.* Compare this experience to the other graphic novels you have read in class this year. Refer to specifics about the experience. In other words, don't just say it was easy or difficult—that's too general.
- Describe the role the media plays in the novel. Why do you think some of the story is told through the television reporters/newscasters? What effect does that have on the way you understand the events in the novel?

- Why do you think Frank Miller includes a new version of Robin in this novel? What is the point of having this particular female Robin in the story?
- Name some of the themes in *Batman: The Dark Knight Returns*. Which is the *most important theme*?
- Can you fight crime effectively without using the same tactics as the criminals? How might Batman respond to this question?
- If V served London as an icon of anarchy, what idea or ideal does Batman embody?
- The battle between Superman and Batman is epic, one of the best battles in comics. How does Superman fit into this particular Batman story? Why does Miller include him at all?
- What makes Batman a "dark character"?
- Do Alan Moore's V and Frank Miller's Batman redefine or challenge the stereotypical definition of a superhero?
- Are Bruce Wayne and Batman one in the same?
- How does the artwork and/or the balance of picture and text in *Batman: The Dark Knight Returns* differ from other graphic novels you have read?

LOOKING AT TEXTUAL CHALLENGES

As students read *Batman: The Dark Knight Returns*, you can expect many questions about the text and several objections. My students were especially troubled by the shifting point of view, flashbacks, and references to former Robin characters, including Jason and Dick Grayson. Brie's response below is an example of the questions that arise from the references to other comic book characters.

On page 177–178 it is pretty unclear what is exactly happening to Clark. I also find it amusing how he looks like he has no bones when he is struck by a magnetic storm. He just looks like a boneless zombie floating around the air. Also, you would assume that after being struck, he would be dead, but somehow, he is alive, and then is rejuvenated by "mother earth". I don't really understand what he's holding on to in the 6th panel on page 178 either. It looks like a sunflower, but for all we know, it could be some gem or something. From that, he just gets up like he wasn't just some freakish zombie and goes off to fight Bruce. It just makes no sense. . . .

Due to a lack of familiarity with the nature of Superman and his ability to be regenerated by the energy of the sun, Brie was momentarily puzzled by the images she was reading. Her comment, "for all we know, it could be some gem or something," suggests that she knows an explanation likely exists but that she does not know what that explanation is. Brie's willingness to persist through this type of ambiguity and remain open-minded to possibilities shows the development of good reading habits. My role as teacher is to provide opportunities for her to record her reading process and learn from it. Brie's issue exemplifies the difficulty that intertextuality poses for inexperienced superhero comics readers.

The structure of Miller's novel is also something students found challenging as it differs from the graphic novels they had recently read. Many pages contain multiple plotlines with constant shifts between them. It takes a great deal of attention to follow the layout of the panels and pages and the colored dialogue boxes. Also, speech balloons indicate a character's thoughts that may or may not reflect the action in the panel. Providing ample time to reread and discuss the troubling aspects of the text, as well as utilizing the more experienced students in the class and referencing secondary resources, helped resolve many of these issues.

Some of the students' more bitter complaints about *Dark Knight Returns* focus on the end of the novel, including the presence of Superman in the story, but this irritation led to greater understanding of Miller's unconventional rendition of the Batman superhero story and the novel's central themes. In his journal, Justin wrote the following in response to items in the text he found annoying.

> Page 131. SUPERMAN? Get your own darn movie and graphic novel. Batman is the dark knight and I hate that [Superman] is in there. Superman should not be in there at all. Enough is enough with corny endings.

I try hard to never disregard a student's reaction, regardless of whether or not it is flat-out complaining. In response to such complaints, a teacher can provide opportunities for students to argue intelligently rather than fall prey to childish whining. Their often negative responses are a great starting point in learning to become authoritative using logical reasoning and evidence, as well as developing a mature voice. Strongly felt responses are also an opportunity for students to learn how to be critical and persuasive, to argue a position, propose new theories, or explore possibilities within a safe classroom community and guided by effective teaching practices. Though I did not pursue this activity with my students, the variety of subjective reactions to Miller's version of a beloved superhero presents a great opportunity for class debate or to develop a lesson for students in which they read professional book reviews and compose their own critique to develop style and voice in writing. Criticism of Miller's artistic choices also provides students with an opportunity to think about alternative ways to construct a superhero narrative, which they eventually apply in the summative writing project at the end of our superhero unit.

WRITING WORKSHOP:
MASTERING THE PARAGRAPH

While students independently complete various writing and artistic responses during their independent reading response activities, analytical writing skills are the focus of our writing workshop. As I defined earlier with regard to our reading workshop, I call our writing processes in class a *workshop* because the work students do is active, constructive, recursive, and generally messy. It is a workshop because it is a place to experiment, apply new (and old) skills and build. In this particular writing workshop, the focus is on the structure and content of a coherent, cohesive paragraph. I conduct mini-lessons to review the logic and organization involved in writing a strong paragraph. The lessons I design focus on the function of topic and concluding sentences, implementing specific word choice, logical relationships between sentences, use of transitional words or phrases, punctuation, and smooth integration of quotes. To this end, I prepare a model reader-response question and response. One of the main objectives in this lesson is to discuss with students why and how a paragraph works as an important tool in communicating one's ideas to others. Since *Batman: The Dark Knight Returns* is so detail rich and packed with such vivid images that stick in reader's minds, it's a great opportunity to help students understand the importance of using specific examples and detail in their writing. Focusing on writing one quality paragraph is an easy way to hone this specific writing skill. The *Batman* paragraph writing lesson is located at the companion website.

COLLABORATIVE WRITING PROJECTS

Implementing collaborative writing projects is an excellent way to foster student dialogue about the process of writing and to witness other writers and artists at work while providing students with the opportunity to practice twenty-first century skills. I require students to use Google Docs and other Web 2.0 tools for developing compositions collaboratively, whether for traditional essay writing or combining pictures and words creatively to convey meaning. These tools allow me to witness students' step-by-step collaboration through the construction of a meaningful piece of writing. I also may hold each student accountable for their individual contributions toward the final product. I can converse and assist in the writing process by working in a shared document with students. They can elicit my help, send me messages, and submit their final papers online as well. Google Docs truly fosters student-centered, process-oriented writing development. In tandem with a graphic novel that promotes so much discussion, I strongly recommend you try using this tool with your students to foster their personal, written expression.

Analytical Essay

As a summative writing assignment, my students have the option to work in groups to write one coherent essay based on a topic of their choice related to their reading and analysis of *Batman: The Dark Knight Returns*. Working further on paragraphing based on our mini-lesson and initial practice, this joint effort allows the students to discuss a topic, develop a thesis through discussion, and divide writing tasks. It also allows the group to evaluate one another's writing technique and style. They are continually discussing, writing, and assessing. It is expected that they will conduct peer review to revise, develop, and edit their work progressively and recursively; focus on transitions and relationships among paragraphs to blend their paragraphs and main ideas; examine word choice and check grammar and mechanics; and organize, revise, and finally publish a finished version. I can track their discussions and progress online and design rubrics to promote quality collaboration or specific aspects of writing. Through discussion of the previous reading response workshop and class discussions (both online and in class), students work together to choose a topic rather than one being assigned to them with a narrow, predetermined rubric. Since so many students react to a variety of topics in Miller's text, I don't want to limit their critical analyses or questioning, though the discussion questions listed in the previous section can serve as useful guides for students struggling to find a writing topic.

Superhero Narrative

When teaching superhero narratives, I also allow students the choice to work individually or collaboratively to compose original superhero narratives in writing, comics, or any combination of visuals and words in order to apply their understanding of the genre. After attempting and failing to write my own fictional story with my students, I recognized that *requiring* a student to write creatively might not be a fair request. This is why it might be a good idea to offer students choice. Both fiction and nonfiction superhero assignments are located at the companion website, in addition to the outstanding visual example of Brielle's superhero mini-comic at the end of this chapter.

CONCLUSION

This chapter shows how using popular culture media and integrating art into the curriculum as part of a secondary school ELA curriculum can effectively promote the development and practice of both traditional and twenty-first century competencies. Because students are so engaged with the action, the vivid images, fantastic plotlines, and unusual reading challenges presented in Miller's text, it seems almost purely pleasurable to students to produce their opinions and reactions to the text in writing or to produce a creative narrative of their own. Although teaching Frank Miller's *Batman: The Dark Knight Returns* might be challenging for most teachers unfamiliar with the superhero comics genre, the critical and creative thinking and composition the text elicits from students is well worth giving it a try. Look at what my students practiced and produced from little more than a glimpse into the world of Batman.

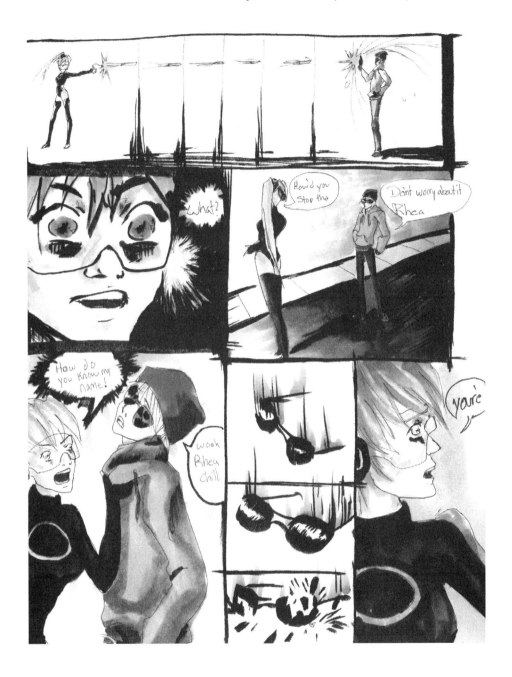

7 Making the Invisible Visible

Alan Moore's *V for Vendetta*

"BEEP! Everybody move to the next panel! Read what's there, comment on what you see, talk about it amongst your group, and add your own contribution to the category. You have seven minutes before moving to the next category. Ready? Go!"

—Ms. Bakis

When my students read *V for Vendetta* by Alan Moore (Moore & Lloyd, 1988), I have to close my classroom door because twenty-eight teenagers moving to the four corners of the classroom and talking can get rather loud. My colleagues across the hall ask me at lunch what the heck I've been up to again. Why would English students be on their feet wandering around the room? What's with all the noise? My answer to that question is that we are busy making sense of *V for Vendetta* and this is best done collaboratively and actively. I must try to keep students' blood pumping in the same way V gets readers' hearts pounding; I must be as equally engaging in the classroom as Moore and Lloyd are with their graphic novel, so the activities I create for students must capture and keep their attention. What I call my Four Corner Category lesson (outlined later in this chapter and found at the companion website) signals the beginning of students' realization that Alan Moore is doing a lot more than what is initially visible to students on the pages of *V for Vendetta*. In other words, this lesson is the beginning of helping students make the invisible visible. Just as V's protégé, Evey, goes from ignorance to enlightenment a la Plato's Allegory of the Cave, so too will students who read *V for Vendetta*.

TEACHABLE TOPICS, CONCEPTS, AND SKILLS

Table 7.1 Teachable Topics, Concepts, and Skills for Alan Moore's *V for Vendetta*

Topics and Concepts	Skills
Elements of story: setting, character, conflict, plot, theme, point of view	Independent reading
Social justice	Group collaboration; online discussion
Violence	Rereading
Art—its nature and cultural significance	Interpretation of words and images
The role of the artist in society	Identifying and applying new knowledge of comics technique (sound, motion, time, color, paneling, word-picture combinations)
Subversion	New vocabulary acquisition; using context clues and resources to learn new terms
Theatre, elements of drama	Oral presentation (small and large group)
Masks	Summarizing information
Symbolism	Writing: response to literature
Metaphor	Note taking: deciphering and recording main ideas and details
Allusion (cultural, historical, literary references)	
Allegory (Plato's Allegory of the Cave)	Identifying literary technique
Irony (dramatic, situational, verbal)	Analysis of text: dialogue, narrative, titles
Closure	Analysis of graphic art: color, lines, panels, gutters
Empathy	Completing closure
Iconography	New vocabulary acquisition; using context clues and resources to learn new terms
Stereotypes	Oral presentation (small and large group)
Freedom versus security	Writing narrative
Survival	Drawing sequential narrative
History (1980s government/cultural concerns in Great Britain, America)	Analytical essay writing

I can't think of a more engaging text to use in the ELA classroom than *V for Vendetta* for both teacher and students. The novel is valuable for its numerous opportunities for explicit skill instruction in reading, including but not limited to the development of new vocabulary, attending to cues in the text, making inferences, examination of narrative structure and organization, and metaphor. *V for Vendetta* can be read and taught using a variety of critical lenses, including formalist, feminist, Marxist, cultural, or historical perspectives. Examples of students' online discussion, writing, and reading along with the various lessons and activities in this chapter, indicate the kind of critical and analytical thinking *V for Vendetta* prompts from students.

V for Vendetta engages, conjures empathy from readers, and speaks to the human condition. Personal and sociopolitical themes in *V for Vendetta* cause readers to consider controversial issues like violence, injustice, and political and moral corruption. The text invites students to visualize themselves in characters' roles and to experience decision making and reactions to fate and events beyond their control. Moore's dystopian fantasy causes students to consider their own moral principles and opinions about government and other socially relevant issues, while also examining satire and persuasion as ways they might express their beliefs to elicit change or to communicate their opinions and concerns. Though constructed in a contemporary format divergent from traditional literature, *V for Vendetta* conjures serious consideration of universal themes like the nature of art, heroes, justice, and good and evil no less effectively than classic, canonical texts. The way *V for Vendetta* generates classroom discussion and lends itself to explicit instruction about the power of art as well as critical media literacy and propaganda are my favorite aspects of teaching this text to high school students.

LOOKING AT REALITY THROUGH FANTASY

Teenagers find *V for Vendetta* appealing because of its fantastic elements, its colorful panels and characters, and its action-packed plot. Within the first few pages of the novel, students are captured by the mysteriousness of the masked iconic V. Students are enthralled by his radical actions, the use of explosives and violence, and the political upheaval his rebelliousness causes. Whether we like it or not, American high school students today have grown up with images of burning towers collapsing following a terrorist strike, easily accessible pornography on the Internet, and television commercials and sitcoms soaked in sexual innuendo that flash before their eyes at an alarming rate. Rather than nostalgically wish for a simpler way of life (or resort to an entirely traditional curriculum) our responsibility as educators is to help students navigate this world, a media-saturated and often violent one. Considering this context, Moore's dystopian world is far from disturbing, but already a familiar part of the American teenage consciousness. Moore's expression of particularly Western cultural fears prevalent in the 1980s can lead to valuable discussion of American teenagers' awareness of terrorism in the post-911 world.

To witness V blowing up statues and buildings or creatively murdering his original torturers at Larkhill allows readers to fantasize about extreme action or what it might feel like to actually carry out a vendetta that moral values and societal norms prohibit. Exploring extremes, while reading *V for Vendetta*, allows students to momentarily press past boundaries without harm. Though it seems safer to force young people into prescribed borders or not let them find out about the worst in this world when they are impressionable and still developing moral and ethical limits, students need to be familiar with what is beyond those boundaries in order to understand the context in which they are negotiating and establishing their own set of behaviors. Mostly, students feel respected that their teacher acknowledges their maturity to handle such imaginative, intellectual, and moral experimenting. Examination of *V for Vendetta*'s characters and conflicts allows students to question or reaffirm their own moral compasses, as well as to understand the influence of environment and social conditioning in shaping lives. Teachers can use *V for Vendetta* to instruct students about the influence of the media and the definition of anarchy, human rights, and individual liberties, and it pairs well with another excellent graphic novel that explores the sometimes desperate dilemma of freedom versus personal security called *Pride of Baghdad* by Brian K. Vaughan (2006).

CONTROVERSIAL IMAGES OR TEACHABLE MOMENTS?

The sexual content, portrayal of women, violence, and Eric Finch's drug use are the more stereotypical problems associated with teaching *V for Vendetta* (though my students did not find them problematic at all but rather interesting issues of analysis and debate), but like any controversial novel, teachers must use these aspects of the texts to responsibly nurture student awareness and learning. For example, a closer examination of the role of women or sex in the novel is an opportunity to introduce students to reading literature critically from a feminist perspective. Whether or not we judge this unfortunate, the controversial aspects of *V for Vendetta* are

part of what makes this text so accessible, engaging, and directly connected to students' experiences outside of school.

The value of art is that it can cause upset or anger as well as instruct
and provide pleasure. *V for Vendetta* is challenging for students and teachers in a number of ways, but that is its inherent value, and I believe, Alan
Moore's intent.

Resolving Textual Challenges

The problems readers experience while reading *V for Vendetta* can be
turned into opportunities for learning. Two subjective-based problems
students experience while reading *V for Vendetta* include the texture of the
paper stock in the 2008 Vertigo edition and the use of color. Some students
feel the coloring is overdone and causes confusion. This problem, however, presents an opportunity to discuss how packaging and form affect
the content of a story and the ability of readers to not only construct meaning as they read but to gain pleasure from this experience. Stressing that
reading is an experience that can be positive or negative is important in
fostering the idea that reading is not merely a school-based performance
but can be enjoyed beyond the classroom for the rest of their lives.

Another problem in the text involves Moore's use of what McCloud
(1993) calls non-sequitur panels and sections of the text that students feel
create too much disjointedness in the narrative flow, interfering with their
comprehension. The number of characters, plotlines, and symbols within
the panels can overwhelm students unfamiliar with superhero comics,
further slowing the pace of reading. This, however, is a good problem as
long as you can convince students to be patient and not rush to finish the
novel as quickly as possible or conversely drag out the reading unneces-
sarily to the point where students lose interest and the narrative becomes
too cryptic, a standard challenge faced by English teachers using any text.
It is in fact far better to encourage students to slow down while reading *V
for Vendetta* in order to grapple with the confusion and complexities within
the text and apply reading strategies.

One of the best "problems" of students reading a complex and challenging text like *V for Vendetta* is the opportunity it presents to reinforce
with students the notion that reading is a process of construction and
reconstruction akin to the writing process. When students stop reading,
this presents an opportunity for identifying weaknesses and problems and
collaborative discussion about what good readers do. By persisting
through some of the ambiguities and challenging aspects of reading *V for
Vendetta*, students are better able to appreciate the variety of literary and
graphic artistry in the text they otherwise might have missed if they quit

reading or carelessly glossed over in an effort to merely get to the end of the story. If you can motivate struggling readers to hang in there, they will be intrigued by what they discover through closer examination of images, dialogue, panel transitions, and action in the gutters.

As is evident in the problems and resolutions above, the role of the teacher is crucial in terms of dealing with the challenges inherent in *V for Vendetta* and not losing less-persistent readers who might feel discouraged by their confusions and be tempted to give up reading altogether. Through question-and-answer discussion sessions and reexamination of panels and narrative, students and teachers can collaborate to clarify initial readings, hear the interpretations of their peers, and work to create social meaning.

FRAMING THE TEXT

I teach *V for Vendetta* in tandem with Frank Miller's *Batman: The Dark Knight Returns* (2002) to introduce students to the traditional aspects of the superhero genre and to examine how Miller and Moore's work challenges that tradition. One of the essential questions for students to consider while reading *V for Vendetta* is whether V fits the traditional definition of a super-hero. My students are already primed to read with this question in mind after viewing the documentary films mentioned in Chapter 6 and reading, writing, and discussing *Batman: The Dark Knight Returns*. I recommend providing the same prereading material used in Chapter 6 for *Batman: The Dark Knight Returns* prior to reading *V for Vendetta* if you can only choose one of these graphic novels for your curriculum.

Prereading Strategies

Before students begin reading, some of the strategies I use to address *V for Vendetta's* complexity include carefully "chunking" the reading for students; reviewing aspects of plot, setting, and character often; and providing secondary resource material to aid students' comprehension. I provide students with a list of character descriptions, an outline of the Norsefire government structure (after they try to figure it out on their own), and biographical information about Guy Fawkes. In addition to the information provided at the companion website (www.corwin.com/graphicnovelclassroom), you can find historical information about Guy Fawkes, the Gunpowder Plot, British government in the 1980s, and a basic overview and analysis of *V for Vendetta* on the Web. Depending on the age of your students, you might have them exercise research skills by finding out about the popular culture and political history in America and Great Britain in the 1980s as a prereading activity.

Looking at Book I

After our initial discussion of heroes and superheroes, students commence reading *V for Vendetta*. When students complete the initial reading and respond in their journals, we review their work during the next class. Students add class notes to their initial journal responses after listening to others and rethinking their initial responses. This is an opportunity for students to check their reading accuracy and clarify initial interpretations about characters, setting, and any other important images or narrative concerns or confusions that occur to them as they read. In addition to the way the journal prompts are designed, this is an opportunity for the teacher to query students about their level of self-awareness and assessment while reading. I use reader response prompts and activities from Jim Burke's *Reading Reminders* (2000). Example questions can include the following.

- How did you reach your conclusion about the setting?
- Which clues in the text led you to determine the time period or place?
- How did you figure out which characters worked for the government and how the government is structured?

Looking at Literary Technique

As students read, they bring their questions and comments to class to share, and as facilitator and guide, I follow their lead.

Some students know that V's recitation from Shakespeare's *Macbeth* beginning on page 12 differs from conventional speech, but they cannot pinpoint the specific reference. A few students recognize it as poetry or iambic pentameter, but most, not having read *Macbeth*, are unable to glean the meaning of the words. Their conversation presents an opportunity for instruction on allusion. The visual references to the Holocaust in Chapter 4 are obvious to most students, whereas the "Life's a stage" (p. 35) comment V offhandedly remarks is completely invisible to students. By making these allusions visible to students, they suddenly realize Moore is doing more than conveying an entertaining plot. I don't tell students how to react to the text or hand them my interpretation of it, but my job is to help them recognize that the cultural and literary references are important in a more detailed understanding of the author's purpose. The allusions also unveil the nature of intertextuality and the importance of being culturally literate. Another important reason to help students understand and appreciate the use of allusion is its value as a potentially useful tool for writing. Additionally, you might have students read the works of the

From *V for Vendetta* (TM) and © DC Comics. All Rights Reserved.

authors Moore references throughout *V for Vendetta*, including William Blake and William Butler Yeats. By recognizing their own lack of experience and understanding of literary conventions, the students not only gain cultural literacy through explication of the allusion, they become more open-minded and attuned to potential discovery of ideas or aspects of text not immediately visible to them upon first read.

Four Corners Category Lesson

After establishing the fact that allusion is one of Moore's important techniques, students are on the lookout for more. To foster close, discriminating reading and delve more deeply into more formal and thematic aspects of the novel, students engage in the Four Corners Category activity with which I introduced this chapter. As the students read independently through Book I of *V for Vendetta* outside of class, in class they work in randomly assigned groups, each of which discusses a topic listed on either block paper or the white board in each corner of the classroom. The categories include: "Literary (and Other) References," "Violence," "Use of V," and "Major Metaphors." Students are asked to write their responses under each topic heading and then move to the next topic at teacher-initiated time intervals. Moving in sequential order across "panels" drawn on the white board or large block paper, students respond to what previous groups note and also add new, original ideas. After groups visit each panel/topic and return to their seats, we review the information collaboratively and take notes. This particular activity fosters both physical and intellectual engagement, reading review and repetition of important concepts wherein students are able to clarify, as a group, initial conclusions based on independent reading. I sometimes repeat the activity during the following class to encourage students to read more actively with the categories in mind. Naturally, you might create your own categories or a variation of this lesson for your own students. I also have implemented this activity for Book III with the categories: motif, vocabulary, endings/resolutions, and allusion.

Looking at Metaphor

Some of the examples of metaphor students identify include Fate as comparable to the fascist regime, the government agencies named after body parts, V's personification of Lady Justice as having betrayed him for another "lover," and the commander's "love affair" with Fate. The major metaphor running throughout the novel is that of theatre. Borrowed from Shakespeare's comedy, *As You Like It*, Moore characterizes V as an actor in the play of life, his role to undo the fascist regime, to unmask the corruption of such a government by way of personal vendetta. The fascist regime is pretense; the government acts righteous, yet masks truth by use of propaganda. The reality of the government's illusion is oppressive, violent dictatorship. The government is "putting on an act" in front of the people, its audience. V constructs a stage, complete with scenes of Larkhill and brings Lewis Prothero, the commander of this former concentration camp, to reenact the horrific killing via incineration he formerly enacted as leader. V burns what is precious to Prothero, his doll collection (toys that resemble *real* people), driving him completely insane. By theatrical reproduction of V's past reality, V's personal vendetta is fulfilled. Moore's use of the vaudeville stage and the cabaret along with a plethora of literary and cultural allusions effectively exhibits a dynamic combination of pulp fiction and classic literature.

Looking at V and Violence

In addition to Moore's use of metaphor and allusion, students find the use of the V symbol entertaining. The list is extensive and illustrator David Lloyd manages to blend the letter *V* into various panels and artwork as well. Students also note the several instances of violence in the novel, which leads to important discussion about the overall meaning of the narrative and Moore's commentary on human nature. When comparing the film with the original text, it is evident that the ways in which V murders his victims changes his characterization and, as a result, the way the audience reacts to and judges him. One of the main questions students grapple with is: Is V a cold-blooded psychopath or is he a vigilante or hero? Looking carefully at his actions and understanding his motivations is imperative to reaching a conclusion about V. V's violent actions also serve as the specific detail in students' written arguments about V. Students also question what means are necessary to exact justice and consider whether V's violence is worse than the fascist regime's resettlement camps. Questions like this that arise from a good piece of literature force students to reconsider their personal values, assumptions, and preconceived notions. This critical thinking leads to intellectual and personal growth. It also reveals the connection between formal technique and content, an important connection for students to realize especially as they create their own authentic texts.

Ideas for Assessment

The quizzes located at the companion website are useful for assessing students' reading of Book I of *V for Vendetta* and to practice writing and peer assessment. I have included an excerpt of the instructions and sample responses from students from a Book I quiz below. Students exchanged their responses, discussed criteria for assessment based on the model paragraph given, and evaluated one another's writing. Much like the quiz on *Persepolis* given in Chapter 4, this quiz can be given to students at any time throughout their reading as it applies to any chapter of the text. I provide students with a list of definitions, but you might very well hand them a dictionary, or blend vocabulary instruction into the assignment.

Paragraph Writing Quiz

As you Voraciously Vault through the pages of the Vortex called V for Vendetta, *please Verify your Version of the meaning of the Very interesting chapter titles in Book I listed below. Please make your writing Vivid and Voluminous using your Very own Voice.*

Explain how each chapter title represents the meaning of the chapter.

- Chapter 2: Voice
- Chapter 4: Vaudeville
- Chapter 11: Vortex

Olivia's Response: In chapter eleven of Alan Moore's V for Vendetta, "The Vortex," at least two vortices are prominently, although none are of the literal variety. The most explicit reference to these vortices comes on page 86, panel 2, when Finch, in reference to V's scheme, says, "You deal with something like this . . . and it's like walking on quicksand. You get slowly sucked into it . . ." On the previous page, he also compares V's scheme to the abstract designs V created with the ammonia and grease solvent in room five (85/9). One can see how V's plan is a sort of vortex—Evey has been sucked into it, and now Finch seems to have become personally involved with it as well. ("I'll see him dead for this," he declares after Dr. Surridge's death (78/4)) By comparison, it is possible to see how Larkhill itself was another kind of vortex—Dr. Surridge, who seemed to have been a good person, was swept into its cycle of cruelty and torture (80–81). V for Vendetta is a series of vortices, all of which interact with each other and which draw others into their depths.

Danny's Response: Chapter 2, "The Voice", in V for Vendetta exhibits the power a single voice can have on the credibility of the government. In this chapter, the reader learns that a man by the name of Lewis is the voice of Fate over the radio. The purpose of Fate "is that people think it's Fate talking. It makes Fate appear more human." (17/4) This shows that the government is using the power of a good speaker, Lewis, as a propaganda weapon to control the masses. Lewis' coworker, Dascombe, even says, "If only people knew what a good job he's doing." (17/3) Chapter 2 is appropriately named because Lewis' voice of "fate" has significant power in the fascist society in which they all live.

LOOKING AT BOOK II

Students work collaboratively throughout Book II to sort through confusions and build social meaning. Because the static nature of comics allows for thorough reexamination, the students sort through and discuss at length the condensed meaning packed into panels and images. This shared activity, both looking together and seeing, keeps students engaged with the text and leads to additional understanding and enjoyment.

Collaborative Close Reading and Discussion Activity

Divide students into groups. I usually make seven groups and ask students to report on two chapters each in Book II of *V for Vendetta*. For example, the first group will review Chapters 1 and 8, the next group will review Chapters 2 and 9, and so on. This activity usually takes two to four class periods to complete and discuss.

Write your answers and be prepared to share with the rest of the class.

1. Tell us what chapter you examined.

2. Please summarize your chapter for the class.

3. Are there any important images or words you noted?

4. Describe any confusion you struggled with in this chapter when you initially read it.

5. How does this chapter relate to the one before it and after it?

6. How does this chapter add to the overall meaning of Book II so far?

7. Identify any continuing patterns including major metaphors, violence, use of V, or allusions (if you mentioned any or all of these in previous answers, you do not have to repeat them here).

Word/Picture Combinations Activity

As part of the Book II group activity above, students also apply comics concepts previously learned from Scott McCloud's *Understanding Comics* (1993) to identify the various word-picture combinations and appropriately cite page numbers and panels according to conventional MLA style requirements.

Directions: After reading and discussing Book II of V for Vendetta, *review Chapter 6, "Show and Tell," in Scott McCloud's* Understanding Comics.

Work in your group to find examples of the following word/picture combinations:

- Word-Specific
- Picture-Specific
- Duo-Specific
- Additive
- Parallel
- Montage
- Interdependent

Think about how form relates to content or how different combinations of words and images affect the meaning of the story.

Plato's Allegory of the Cave

After students read Book II of *V for Vendetta*, we read and discuss Plato's Allegory of the Cave, using it as a metaphor for understanding Evey's transformation and to reinterpret V's television broadcast to Londoners. I ask students to step back from the novel and consider it as a whole to this point in light of Plato's allegory. We also revisit and reconsider Moore's letter at the beginning of the novel to think about the purpose of *V for Vendetta*, the comics medium, and the author and illustrator's technique employed thus far. Using Plato's Allegory of the Cave with *V for Vendetta* with my teenage students is valuable in moving them beyond overly simplified interpretations of this novel and by extension, other texts they read. Their ideas of analysis are sometimes limited to reductionist interpretations or merely naming the "moral of the story," but *V for Vendetta*, however, can be used to teach students that a lot more is going on in a text than meets the eye and that sometimes an author's purpose cannot be so easily simplified as they would like. Motivating students to move beyond contentedness with a simplistic interpretation used merely to have something to write about and receive a participation grade for is important. This problem is related to the conditioning of traditional forms of learning where students perform, often thoughtlessly, to fulfill achievement goals that have been set by others. The themes and characters in *V for Vendetta* can prompt the kind of discussion that may enlighten students and foster authentic forms of learning beyond the desire for a "good grade."

LOOKING AT BOOK III

As mentioned earlier, I use the Four Corners category lesson with students as a way of exploring Book III of *V for Vendetta*. I also quiz students on

Book III to assess their comprehension and reading strategies. The quiz questions are located at the companion website and also might serve as discussion prompts. Discussions I initiate in class with students include the role of art in society, its subversive nature and its manipulation, as well as the influence of artists on the development of Western culture. Students further examine *V for Vendetta* in their online discussion forum. Below you will find example student responses to give you an idea about the type of conversations that occur among students about *V for Vendetta*. Allowing students control over their own discussions is invaluable for encouraging more democratic and independent thinking among students. It is also good writing practice for a real audience. Discussion forum prompts are located at the companion website.

Sample Student Discussion Thread 1

Started by Kailey: Is V moral? I think V has good intentions but I think he could get revenge in more humane ways; two wrongs do not make a right. I originaly thought that V was more good than evil but after he abandoned Evey I realized that his need for revenge at all cost made him more of a villian than a hero. I do not blame him for seeking revenge, and I don't think he really cares if people see him as a hero or not because he is not trying to be a hero to the popele, he is trying to get revenge on the government for the containment camps and as long as he gets revenge he couldn't care less of what the people think of him.

Reply by Liz: I agree! V's violence and revenge has gone a little too far.

Reply by Ali: I think that V is moral is his own mind. If the story about his experience in room 5 is true, then I believe he went entire insane. He now lives in a world where he is the ultimate justice in a world or corruption and evil. To him, he is the savior of this world and it his job to rid it of anything he sees as a danger.

Sample Student Discussion Thread 2

Started by Ali: I was wondering if anyone else was bothered by the fact we have no clue if anything in "Vortex" was true. The chapter ends with a lingering thought that "V could've fabricated the entire story," and none if it was true. I'm lead to believe it is at least partially true that there was at least a person that survived in room five, due to the reaction of Fate when V showed him the door. But it's making me wonder if we'll ever know where he actually came from.

Reply by Katie: I also didn't think about the truth to his story. I believe that the story is true but I am open to other opinions. The reason I think the story is true is because the Dr. wrote about him in her diary. It also fits the story line and helps us understand why he would torture Evey. There are also hints here and there of his experience. For example, Evey finds the five page letter in her cell and it was real. Although it could also be argued that V wrote it.

The students' discussion threads show the challenging aspects of *V for Vendetta* and their efforts to resolve them through dialogue.

While online, a few students added links to YouTube videos featuring interviews with Alan Moore, one of which I showed in class after we finished reading *V for Vendetta*. Other students, as part of their discussion, added links to news stories and other media where *V for Vendetta* is referenced. Using culturally relevant texts with social networking in the classroom is a powerful combination that fosters authentic discussion from students and more engaged learning.

Considering Endings

I ask students throughout their reading of *V for Vendetta* to consider whether or not V is a hero or a villain, and students are challenged to consider their own moral values about justice in addition to their notions of society and government in light of their new reading experience. Great argument ensues among students about heroism, superheroes, justice, and vigilantism as they read *V for Vendetta*, allowing teachers to develop lessons involving debate. The end of the novel also allows students to develop interesting theories about why Moore ends with the final image of Finch with his back to the reader walking down a long, empty road out of London after having thwarted Helen Heyer, who continuously lobbies him to join her in a desperate attempt to regain power. Students also make predictions about what will happen in London next and trade ideas about a sequel to *V for Vendetta*, suggesting additional classroom projects. The end of the book also raises the discussion of whether V really dies and the distinction between the man under the mask versus the idea. Since V is iconic, this is yet another opportunity to reference our previous concepts of icons learned from Scott McCloud's *Understanding Comics*. We also discuss how the final plotlines come to closure, including Rosemary, Eric Finch, and the "vultures," all of which leads to further clarification, interpretation, and reconsideration of the entire narrative. Since *V for Vendetta*'s multilayered visual and narrative format invites an extensive array of activities, teachers and students could spend many months engaged with this text in the classroom.

Insight Into the Creative Process

"Behind the Painted Smile" is an article written by Alan Moore found at the end of *V for Vendetta* (2008) that gives insight into the artistic process of creating *V for Vendetta*. Moore recounts the chronology of events leading to *V for Vendetta* as a finished product. This piece models for students an ability to reflect on the origination of ideas, characterization, consideration of form and audience, as well as other aspects of the process of creating a graphic novel, invaluable information to inform their own composition. I typically assign the reader response questions below for homework, but a more extensive list of response and discussion questions can be found at the companion website.

1. Show you read and understood the essay by describing Alan Moore's tone, using proof from the article to support your response.

2. Briefly summarize the purpose and audience of "Behind the Painted Smile."

3. What surprised you about what you read?

4. What did you find most interesting about this essay?

5. What did you learn about the collaborative relationship between artist and author from this article?

Same Story in a Different Medium?

I show students the Warner Brothers film version of *V for Vendetta* (McTeigue, 2006) and ask them to compare the story told in different media formats. Alan Moore has strong opinions about the relationship between the graphic novel medium and film, some of which we read about or listen to (see BBC Comics Britannia, 2007) on YouTube in class. I also ask students to read and respond to Nicholas Xenakis' (2006) critique of the film version of *V for Vendetta*. This article also serves as a model for writing their critiques of choice novels as part of another independent reading project being conducted simultaneously.

Creative and Analytical Composition

I have used two different composition assignments for students to practice writing after reading *V for Vendetta*. An analytical essay challenges students to write about *V for Vendetta* using suggested prompts. A number of the topics listed are based on student inquiries and our various conversations and activities throughout the unit. Though I provide students with possible topics, I encourage them to take the opportunity to flesh out their own ideas and personal reactions that develop as a result of their genuine and personal engagement with the story. In addition to the essay writing prompts, the writing workshop models related to *V for Vendetta* are located at the companion website.

As mentioned in Chapter 6, I also have included a creative writing assignment that gives students an opportunity to compose in the superhero genre in order for them to gain a better appreciation for it. Teenagers do not often get space or time in school to explore innovative ideas and develop purely entertaining stories, so those who have an affinity for creativity thrive with this assignment. In addition to Brielle's superhero story located at the end of Chapter 6, page one of Samantha's mini superhero story here is evidence of the amazing sequential art narrative students can create if given the space and time.

CONCLUSION

Since *V for Vendetta* (and many other graphic novels) appeals to and entertains students, it is far easier to engage them in collaborative learning activities, further discovery of the layers of meaning they may not have originally recognized in their private reading, and application of new literary and comics techniques. It is far more difficult to facilitate skills practice and knowledge acquisition if important lessons remained buried within the pages of an unopened book on the desks of disinterested students.

Afterword

The Value of Teaching Graphic Novels

Many teachers justify the use of graphic novels in the classroom because of their companionable thematic content with other classic works of literature, yet treat form as a secondary consideration by perhaps thinking graphic art and other forms of media involving images is best left to the art department. I did too, but I soon realized that graphic novels' value in developing literacy skill lies in the examination of the formal aspects of the medium. And I don't mean incidentally looking at nice visuals that accompany the narrative; I mean really reading images deeply and as part of the language of the medium.

By teaching visual literacy, my students report that they are now better, more discriminating and self-aware readers than they were before they started reading graphic novels. In addition to discussions of character, conflict, theme, and setting, students in the graphic novel classroom also talk about images, icons, and how we know and interpret what we see. We talk about perception and making assumptions, and we challenge preconceptions. We talk about the influences on the way we see and read and how one reaches consensus or conclusions about stories told in sequential art form. We explore content and form as inextricable. Best of all, students realize that there are more ways to express themselves and tell stories beyond printed words on paper, and they experience success and personal satisfaction in experimenting communicating using images in a graphic novel classroom.

POWERFUL WORDS AND IMAGES

I want to leave you with a few final powerful words and images from the students' end of the course portfolio assignment where they were asked simply to write about and draw what they learned in the graphic novel classroom.

> *"My whole life growing up I've hated reading, but since I have been reading graphic novels I have finally found a kind of book I actually enjoy reading."*
>
> —Craig

> *"After taking this class I have learned that I can take a lot away from something unexpected. This class has shown me that trying something out of the ordinary can be surprisingly beneficial and could stay with you for the rest of your life. The graphic novel course has influenced me to try new things in life and be open-mined to different ideas."*
>
> —D. J.

> *"This class has prepared me for college because it has made me think in ways I have never been made to think. I am more observant and I have become aware of the value and significance of what can be perceived visually."*
>
> —Robbie

> *"Graphic Novel struck me as something new, fun, and exciting. This class was a breath of fresh air . . . I loved that we had a chance to come up with our own ideas and weren't on a tight leash when it came to projects like designing our own graphic novel. Thank you for creating this class and showing people that there is more than one way to read book[s] and learn English!"*
>
> —Liz

When I was a kid I always struggled to read. Though I loved stories and books, I only like listening to my mom read them to me.

I grew to hate reading. It was purely frustrating and tiring. I rarely read books for pleasure, and never read books for school.

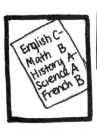   

This past summer I got diagnosed with dyslexia.

My English grades were decent for the majority of my schooling, but as I grew up my classes got harder and my grade suffered.

When I picked my classes for this year I kept my hatred for reading in mind. I have always loved art and I thought that combining art and English, with graphic novels would be the perfect course for me.

I have learned many things this year. I have learned to love many books including A Contract with God, Maus, and Persepolis.

I have learned to read images and dialogue fluidly, and I have also learned how to use media to both collaborate with group members and share my own opinions.

This class has been beneficial for me, and I cannot wait to use what I have learned in my future. —Helen

"I've spent years reading all text books, and while I still do, it was interesting that I could be reading a format that some consider childish in school, when at home I would be reading technical publications and philosophical titles. It was bizarre that I would spend so much time analyzing a comic book and breeze through a report on string theory."

—Ali

"The reason I didn't like normal lit in other English classes is because I never got images in my head when I read books, and it was more difficult for me to stay reading a book than it was for other students. And in graphic novel[s] there are already pictures, but you still need to put motion to them using your imagination. I found this really fun

because everyone knows that the characters get from point A to point B, but everyone has a different way of getting there through the panels."

—Ryan

"I am not very fond of reading, so I enjoyed this class because I was able to read an entire book and not become bored with the text. We were able to cover more material. . . . This class required more interaction than any other English class I have endured. No longer did reading consist of solely words, rows of letters that blurred into rows of black lines on white paper . . . while you read you have to also study the images that correspond with the words. This made me slow down and take my time when reading rather than rush through extensive amounts of words."

—Jane

"Learning about graphic storytelling and about reading graphic novels has helped me pay attention to details of writing and imagery, not just words. . . . This class has helped me to prepare for college by exposing me to new ideas and forcing me to go out of my comfort zone."

—Josh

"I learned that the graphic medium has the power to change one's perspective completely about literature. . . . I now know that written language is not the only way for an author to portray his or her perspective."

—Matt

"The most positive learning experience . . . came from the Scott McCloud book . . . it made the comics medium and how it works very clear and understandable. After reading that book I was able to analyze other books that I read more accurately. I understood what I was reading and took into account the structure and importance of the images. I found that the medium is extremely unique . . . [comics] utilizes all the senses of the reader and make the story that much better to read creating a better reading experience. . . . During this course I learned how to think about how I read while I'm actually reading."

—Jake

"I learned that knowledge gained from literature is unlimited. Writing in general is a collective representation of the human soul, never-ending, and chock full of individual voices that want to be heard.

Graphic novels are no less important of a portrayal of personal expression than fully worded novels. Everyone is afraid, not so much of death, but the idea of being forgotten. It is in our nature to desire immortality in some form (a little something I picked up from this class). It is important that we learn all different mediums of expression, or else we may never be heard. There is something capturing about graphic novels, to see the story in the way the writer intended—to see reality through someone else's eyes. There is something more real about static images, something that holds your attention and screams, listen! See my hardship, see my joy—make sense of it, and know that you are not alone."

—Laura

Resources

GRAPHIC NOVEL EDUCATOR RESOURCES

GraphicNovelsandHighSchoolEnglish.com

The Graphic Novel Classroom author, Maureen Bakis, welcomes graphic novel enthusiasts to read, blog, and discuss teaching using comics on this social network. Resources related to teaching and learning with graphic novels are housed on the site, including group discussions listed by novel title, event updates, articles, and RSS feeds. An extensive list of links on the homepage lead to comics scholars and artists' blogs and websites, as well as comics creation tools and publishers websites. Many of the links and resources cited in *The Graphic Novel Classroom* are archived at this site.

School Library Journal's Good Comics for Kids

The world's largest reviewer of books, multimedia, and technology for children and teens, this site provides informed reviews from experienced graphic novel specialists and rich resources about comics, graphic novels, and manga. (http://blog.schoollibraryjournal.com/goodcomicsforkids/)

American Library Association (ALA) Young Adult Library Services Association (YALSA) Annual Great Graphic Novels for Teens

Great Graphic Novels for Teens is a list of recommended graphic novels and illustrated nonfiction for those ages 12 to 18, prepared yearly by YALSA. (http://www.ala.org/ala/mgrps/divs/yalsa/booklistsawards/greatgraphicnovelsforteens/gn.cfm)

ALA: Dealing With Challenges to Graphic Novels

This page offers tips to help you prepare for challenges to using graphic novels in your school. (http://www.ala.org/Template.cfm?Section=ifissues&Template=/ContentManagement/ContentDisplay.cfm&ContentID=130336)

TeachingComics.org: Comics Educators and Resources

Teachingcomics.org is the homepage of the National Association of Comics Art Educators (NACAE). The site is a resource where educators in comic art and sequential art can get and share ideas.

Citations Guide for Graphic Novels and Comics

This citations guide will assist you with formatting issues related to scholarly writing about comics. (http://www.comicsresearch.org/CAC/cite.html)

DiamondBookshelf.com

Find testimonials, lesson ideas, book lists, reviews, and articles about teaching graphic novels and comics in the classroom.

GraphicNovelReporter.com

Subscribe to the GNR newsletter to get the latest updates about the comics industry; new titles; author, artist, and teacher interviews; op-eds; and comic convention news and other national events. The site hosts everything and anything related to graphic novels.

SUGGESTED READING FOR TEACHING GRAPHIC NOVELS

Will Eisner's *Graphic Storytelling and Visual Narrative* (2008), originally published in 1996 by W.W. Norton, is an excellent resource for teachers to read before teaching comics and for younger students who may not be ready to read McCloud's *Understanding Comics* (1993).

Will Eisner's *Comics and Sequential Art: Principles and Practices From the Legendary Cartoonist* (W.W. Norton, 2008) is another excellent resource for understanding and applying the principles of the comics medium.

Hollis Margaret Rudiger's "Reading Lessons: Graphic Novels 101" is an excellent article published in the April/May, 2006 issue of *The Horn Book Magazine* (pp. 126–134). If you don't have time to teach Eisner or McCloud's texts listed above, you might use this short article, which literally walks the reader through the process of reading comics in a simple, straightforward way. This is a perfect resource for a workshop.

Nancy Frey & Douglas Fischer's *Teaching Visual Literacy,* published in 2008 by Corwin, is an edited collection of chapters from educators using comics, graphic novels, and other media in their classrooms to promote learning how to better communicate using images. The authors' introduction provides crucial information about understanding importance of visual literacy in the twenty-first century.

Dr. James Bucky Carter's *Building Literacy Connections With Graphic Novels: Page by Page, Panel by Panel,* published by the National Council of Teachers of English (NCTE) in 2007, contains a collection of chapters based on teachers' experiences using graphic novels at the secondary education level.

Dr. James Bucky Carter's *Rationales for Teaching Graphic Novels,* published in 2010, is an edited compilation of work from numerous educators nationwide and is a tremendous resource not only for providing rationales but for its information about more than 100 graphic novels. The DVD list of titles is alphabetized and includes suggestions for braiding, reviews, possible objections, awards, links to resources, and lesson ideas.

Dr. Katie Monnin's *Teaching Graphic Novels: Practical Strategies for the Secondary ELA Classroom,* published by Maupin House in 2010, provides unique strategies for teaching middle and high school language arts students how to read graphic novels.

Stephen Tabachnick's *Teaching the Graphic Novel,* an edited collection of articles published by the Modern Language Association of America in 2009, provides ideas for teaching graphic novels in upper grade levels of secondary education, undergraduate, and graduate level courses from experienced graphic novel educators.

What It Is by Lynda Barry, published in 2008 by Drawn & Quarterly, is an interesting and creative resource that explores the purpose of art and storytelling in a collage-based format.

Scott McCloud's *Making Comics: Storytelling Secrets of Comics, Manga, and Graphic Novels,* published by Harper Paperbacks in 2006, is a helpful resource for learning the various techniques for creating your own comics.

Dr. Michael Bitz's *When Commas Meet Kryptonite: Classroom Lessons From the Comic Book Project* illustrates the incredible success kids experience through creating their own comic books with ideas for helping your students do the same.

Matt Madden and Jessica Abel's *Drawing Words and Writing Pictures: Making Comics: Manga, Graphic Novels, and Beyond,* published by First Second in 2008, contains a plethora of mini-lessons and activities for basic cartooning. The authors' knowledge of and emphasis on the basic principles of storytelling are incredibly helpful for language arts teachers at all levels of education.

Graphic Novels for Secondary ELA Classroom Use

Briggs, R. (1998). *Ethel & Ernest: A true story.* New York: Alfred A. Knopf.

Chabon, M. (2000). *The amazing adventures of Kavalier & Clay.* New York: Picador.

Clowes, D. (2007). *Ghost world.* Seattle: Fantagraphics Books.

Gaiman, N. (2010). *The best American comics 2010.* New York: Houghton Mifflin Harcourt.

Guibert, E., Didier L., & Lemercier, F. (2009). *The photographer* (A. Siegel, Trans.). New York: First Second.

Hamilton, T. (2009). *Ray Bradbury's Fahrenheit 451: The authorized adaptation.* New York: Hill & Wang.

Jacobson, S., & Colon, E. (2006). *The 911 report: A graphic adaptation.* New York: Hill & Wang.

Jacobson, S., & Colon, E. (2010). *The Anne Frank house authorized graphic biography.* New York: Hill & Wang.

Kuper, P., & Kafka, F. (2003). *The metamorphosis.* New York: Crown.

Mazzucchelli, D. (2009). *Asterios polyp.* New York: Pantheon.

Moore, A. (1987). *Watchmen.* New York: DC Comics.

Pekar, H. (1986). *American splendor: Ordinary life is pretty complex stuff.* New York: Ballantine.

Sacco, J. (2000). *Safe area Gorazde: The war in eastern Bosnia, 1992–1995.* Seattle: Fantagraphics Books.

Small, D. (2009). *Stitches: A memoir.* New York: W.W. Norton.

Spiegelman, A. (2004). *In the shadow of no towers.* New York: Pantheon Books.

Thompson, C. (2006). *Blankets.* Marietta, GA: Top Shelf Productions.

Vaughn, B. (2006). *Pride of Baghdad.* New York: DC Comics.

Ware, C. (2000). *Jimmy Corrigan: The smartest kid on earth.* New York: Pantheon Books.

White, T. (2010). *How I made it to eighteen.* New York: Roaring Brook Press.

Winick, J. (2000). *Pedro and me: Friendship, loss, and what I learned.* New York: Henry Holt.

References and Further Reading

Alvermann, D. E., & Hagood, M. C. (2000). Critical media literacy: Research, theory, and practice in "new times." *Journal of Educational Research, 93*(3), 193–205.

Andrasick, K. (1990). *Opening texts.* Portsmouth, N.H.: Heinemann.

Atwell, N. (1998). *In the middle: New understandings about writing, reading and learning* (2nd ed.). Portsmouth, NH: Heinemann.

Abel, J., & Madden, M. (2008). *Drawing words & writing pictures: Making comics: manga, graphic novels, and beyond.* New York: First Second.

BBC Comics Britannia. (2007, October 14). Alan Moore talks - 01 - V for Vendetta. Retrieved from http://www.youtube.com

Bitz, M. (2004). The comic book project: Forging alternative pathways to literacy. *Journal of Adolescent and Adult Literacy, 47*(7), 574–586.

Bitz, M. (2010). *When commas meet kryptonite: Classroom lessons from the comic book project.* New York: Teachers College Press.

Blau, S. (2003). *The literature workshop: Teaching texts and their readers.* Portsmouth, NH: Heinemann.

Boatright, Michael D. (2010). Graphic journeys: Graphic novels' representations of immigrant experiences: Graphic novels can be a provocative resource for engaging the complex issues surrounding immigrant experiences. *Journal of Adolescent and Adult Literacy, 53*(6), 468–469.

Boyne, J. (2006). *The boy in the striped pajamas.* New York: David Fickling Press.

Brodsky, L. (2010, May). The art of teaching an essential list. *GraphicNovelReporter.com.* Retrieved from http://graphicnovelreporter.com

Burke, J. (1999). *The English teacher's companion.* Portsmouth, NH: Boynton-Cook.

Burke, J. (2000). *Reading reminders: Tools, tips, and techniques.* Portsmouth, NH: Heinemann.

Burke, J. (2010). *What's the big idea: Question-drive units to motivate reading, writing, and thinking.* Portsmouth, NH: Heinemann.

Carrier, D. (2000). *The aesthetics of comics.* University Park: The Pennsylvania State University Press.

Carter, J. (2007). *Building literacy connections with graphic novels: Page by page, panel by panel.* Urbana, IL: National Council of Teachers of English (NCTE).

Daniels, L. (1975). *Comix: A history of comic books in America.* New York: Bonanza.

Daniels, L. (1995). *DC Comics: Sixty years of the world's favorite comic book heroes.* Boston: Little, Brown.

Diamond Bookshelf. (2008). Graphic storytelling and the new literacies: An interview with NCTE educator Peter Gutiérrez. *Diamond Bookshelf.* Retrieved from http://www.diamondbookshelf.com

Eisner, W. (2006a). *A contract with god.* New York: W. W. Norton.

Eisner, W. (2006b). *A life force.* New York: W. W. Norton.

Eisner, W. (2008). *Graphic storytelling and visual narrative: Principles and practices from the legendary cartoonist.* New York: W. W. Norton.

English, C. (2007, September). Finding a voice in a threaded discussion group: Talking about literature online. *English Journal, 97*(1), pp. 56–61. Retrieved from http://www.ncte.org/journals/ej

Fingeroth, D. (2004). *Superman on the couch: What superheroes really tell us about ourselves and our society.* New York: Continuum.

Fischer, D., & Frey, N. (2004). Using graphic novels, anime, and the internet in an urban high school. *English Journal, 93*(3), 19–25. Retrieved from http://www.ncte.org/journals/ej

Fisher, D., & Frey, N. (2008). *Visual literacy.* San Diego: Corwin.

Fisher, D., & Frey, N. (2010). Graphic novels: Composing with sequential art in high school English and history. *The NERA Journal, 45*(2), 9–15.

Fulwiler, T. (Ed.). (1987). *The journal book.* Portsmouth, NH: Boynton Cook/Heinemann.

Gallagher, K. (2004). *Deeper reading: Comprehending challenging texts, 4–12.* Portland, ME: Stenhouse.

Gallagher, K. (2009). *Readicide: How schools are killing reading and what you can do about it.* Portland, ME: Stenhouse.

Garnsey, M. (Producer). (2009, November 9). A death in Tehran. [Television series episode]. *Frontline.* Boston: WGBH/Frontline. Retrieved from http://www.pbs.org/wgbh/pages/frontline

Gillenwater, C. (2009). Lost literacy: How graphic novels can recover visual literacy in the literacy classroom. *Afterimage, 37*(2), 33–36.

Gillenwater, C. (2010). The social nature of graphic novels: An interview with Cary Gillenwater. *Diamond Bookshelf, 5,* 18–19.

Glidden, S. (2010). *How to understand Israel in 60 days or less.* New York: Vertigo.

Gornick, V. (2001). *The situation and the story: The art of personal narrative.* New York: Farrar Straus & Giroux.

Griffith, P. E. (2010). Graphic novels in the secondary classroom and school libraries. *Journal of Adolescent and Adult Literacy, 54*(3), 181–189.

Gutierrez, P. (2010, November). Building better readers with graphic storytelling. [Web log message]. Retrieved from http://graphicclassroom.blogspot.com/2010/11/building-better-readers-with-graphic.html

Hassett, D. D., & Schieble, M. B. (2007). Finding space and time for the visual in K–12 literacy instruction. *English Journal, 97*(1), 62–68.

Herman, M. (Director). (2008). *The boy in the striped pajamas* [Motion picture]. United States: Mirimax

Hess, F. M. (2008). The new stupid. *Educational Leadership, 66*(4), 12–17.

Hill, C. (n.d.). Practicing text-image relationships. National Association of Comics Art Educators website. Retrieved from http://www.teachingcomics.org

Ito, M., Horst, H. A., Bittani, M., Boyd, D., Herr-Stephenson, B., Lange, . . . Robinson, L. (2008, November). *Living and learning with new media: Summary of findings from the digital youth project* [White paper]. The MacArthur Foundation. Cambridge: MIT Press.

Jacobson, S., & Colon, E. (2006). *The 911 report: A graphic adaptation.* New York: Hill & Wang.

Jacobson, S., & Colon, E. (2010). *The Anne Frank house authorized graphic biography.* New York: Hill & Wang.

Karr, M. (2005). *The liars' club.* New York: Penguin.

Karr, M. (2009). *Lit.* New York: Harper.

Keene, E. O., & Zimmerman, S. (1997). *Mosaic of thought: Teaching comprehension in a reader's workshop.* Portsmouth, NH: Heinemann.

Kist, W. (2010). *The socially networked classroom: Teaching in the new media age.* Thousand Oaks, CA: Corwin.

Kreis, S. (2000). Plato, the allegory of the cave. *The history guide: Lectures on modern European intellectual history.* Retrieved from http://www.historyguide.org/intellect/allegory.html

Kroopnick, S. (Director) (2003). *Comic book superheroes unmasked* [Video]. United States: Triage Entertainment.

Larson, L. C. (2009). Reader response meets new literacies: Empowering readers in online learning communities. *The Reading Teacher, 62*(8), 638–648.

Lee, S., & Perlman, R. (2008, November 4). *Starz inside: Comic books unbound* [DVD]. United States: Foglight Entertainment.

Letter from Tehran: Veiled Threat. (2009, October 5). *The New Yorker*, pp. 38–42.

Leu, D. J., Jr. (2002). The new literacies: Research on reading instruction with the internet. In A. E. Farstrup & S. J. Samuels (Eds.). *What research says about reading instruction* (pp. 310–336). Newark, DE: International Reading Association.

MacDonell, C. (2004). Making the case for pleasure reading. *Teacher Librarian, 31*(4), 30–32.

Masilimani, R. (2007). Two kinds of people. In R. DiYanni (Ed.), *Literature: Reading fiction, poetry, and drama* (6th ed., pp. 312–317). New York: McGraw-Hill.

McCloud, S. (1993). *Understanding comics: The invisible art.* New York: Harper Collins.

McCloud, S. (2005). Scott McCloud on comics [Video]. Retrieved from http://www.ted .com

McPherson, K. (2006). Literacy links: Graphic literacy. *Teacher Librarian, 33*(4), 67–69.

McTeigue, J. (Director). (2006). *V for vendett*a. [Motion picture]. United States: Warner Brothers Pictures.

Miller, F. (2002). *Batman: The dark knight returns.* New York: DC Comics.

Monnin, K. (2010). *Teaching graphic novels: Practical strategies for the secondary ELA classroom.* Gainseville, FL: Maupin House.

Moore, A., & Lloyd, D. (1988). *V for vendetta.* New York: DC Comics.

Moore, A., & Lloyd, D. (2008). *V for vendetta.* New York: DC Comics.

Motoko, R. (2009, August). The future of reading: A new assignment: Pick books you like. *New York Times*, p. A1. Retrieved from http://www.nytimes.com/2009/08/30/ books/30Reading.html

National Council of Teachers of English. (2005, September). Using comics and graphic novels in the classroom. *The Council Chronicle.* Retrieved from http://www.ncte.org/ magazine/archives/122031

National Council of Teachers of English and Internationl Reading Association. (1996). *The standards for the English language arts.* Retrieved from http://www.ncte.org/standards.

Nolan, C. (Director). (2005). *Batman begins.* [Motion picture]. United States: Warner Bros. Pictures.

Nolan, C. (Director). (2008). *The dark knight* [Motion picture]. United States: Warner Bros. Pictures.

Panella, B. (2004, September) Graphic novels: The POW-er in the classroom. *Diamond Bookshelf.* Retrieved from http://www.diamondbookshelf.com

Partnership for 21st Century Skills. (2009, December). P21 framework definitions. Retrieved from http://www.p21.org

PBS Newshour. (2010). *Governing Iran: Key events in Iran since 1921.* Retrieved from http:// www.pbs.org/newshour/indepth_coverage/middle_east/iran/timeline.html

PBS Teachers. (2002). Elie Wiesel: First person singular. Retrieved from http://www.pbs .org/eliewiesel/

Pedler, M. (2010, December). An interview with Sarah Glidden. Retrieved from http:// www.bookslut.com/features/2010_12_016913.php

Putz, M. (2006). *A teacher's guide to the multi-genre project: Everything you need to get started.* Portsmouth, NH: Heinemann.

Reidelbach, M. (1991). *Completely MAD: A history of the comic book and magazine.* Boston: Little, Brown.

Robbins, T. (1999). *From girls to grrrlz: A history of women's comics from teens to zines.* San Francisco: Chronicle Books.

Rosenblatt, L. (1978). *The reader, the text, the poem: The transactional theory of the literary work.* Carbondale: Southern Illinois University Press.

Rosenblatt, L. (1995). *Literature as exploration* (5th ed.). New York: Modern Language Association of America.

Sabin, R. (1996). *Comics, comix & graphic novels*. London: Phaidon Press.

Sanders, S. R. (1989). Under the influence: Paying the price of my father's booze. *Harpers*, (November), 68–75.

Satrapi, M., & Paronnaud, V. (Directors). (2007). *Persepolis* [Motion picture]. United States: Sony Pictures Classics.

Satrapi, M. (2004). *Persepolis: The story of a childhood*. New York: Pantheon.

Satrapi, M. (2005). *Persepolis: The story of a return*. New York: Pantheon.

Schwarz, G. E. (2002). Graphic novels for multiple literacies. *Journal of Adolescent & Adult Literacy, 46*(3), 262–265.

Seabrook, A. (Correspondent). (2004, June). Interview: Danny Fingeroth discusses why people like superheroes so much as told in his book *Superman on the couch* [Radio series broadcast]. In *Weekend All Things Considered*. Washington DC: National Public Radio. Retrieved from http://www.npr.org

Smiley, T. (Host). (2008, January 17). Marjane Satrapi. In *Tavis Smiley* [Television series broadcast]. Los Angeles: The Smiley Group. Retrieved from http://www.pbs.org

Spiegelman, A. (1986). *Maus I: A survivor's tale: My father bleeds history*. New York: Pantheon.

Spiegelman, A. (1991). *Maus II: A survivor's tale: And here my troubles began*. New York: Pantheon.

Spiegelman, A. (in press). *MetaMaus: A Look Inside a Modern Classic*. New York: Pantheon.

Stamburg, S. (Correspondent). (2004, January 26). Intersections: Of "Maus" and Spiegelman: "MAD" inspired comic book look at the holocaust [Radio series broadcast]. In E. McDonnell (Executive producer), *Morning Edition*. Washington DC: National Public Radio. Retrieved from http://www.npr.org

Success Stories: Testimonials from Teachers and Librarians. (2009). *Diamond Bookshelf*. Retrieved from http://www.diamondbookshelf.com/public/default.asp?t=2&m=1&c=20&s=178.

Tabachnick, S. E. (2007). A comic book world. *World Literature Today, 81*(2), 24–28.

Tabachnick, S. E. (Ed.). (2009). *Teaching the graphic novel*. New York: Modern Language Association of America.

Tan, S. (2006). *The arrival*. New York: Scholastic.

Toomey, J. P. (2010, August 25). Learning from Sherman, the talking shark: Jim Toomey on TED.com. Retrieved from http://ted.com

Vaughn, B. (2006). *Pride of Baghdad*. New York: DC Comics.

Ware, C. (2009, November 2). Unmasked. *The New Yorker*, pp. 84–87.

Weiner, S. (2004). Show, don't tell: Graphic novels in the classroom. *English Journal, 94*(2), 114–117.

West, K. C. (2008). Weblogs and literary response: Socially situated identities and hybrid social languages in English class blogs. *Journal of Adolescent and Adult Literacy, 51*(7), 588–598.

Wiesel, E. (2006). *Night*. New York: Hill & Wang.

Wiesel, E. (2008, April 7). This I believe: A god who remembers. [Radio series broadcast]. In *All Things Considered*. Washington DC: National Public Radio. Retrieved from http://www.npr.org

Wright, B. (2000). Batman. In S. Pendergast & T. Pendergast (Eds.), *St. James encyclopedia of popular culture, Vol. 1* (pp. 189–191). Detroit: St. James Press.

Wright, B. W. (2001). *Comic book nation: The transformation of youth culture in America*. Baltimore: Johns Hopkins University Press.

Xenakis, N. (2006). T for terrorist. *The National Interest, 84*(Summer), pp. 134–138. Retrieved from http://findarticles.com

Yang, G. L. (2008). *American born Chinese*. New York: Square Fish.

Index

CORWIN

A SAGE Company

The Corwin logo—a raven striding across an open book—represents the union of courage and learning. Corwin is committed to improving education for all learners by publishing books and other professional development resources for those serving the field of PreK–12 education. By providing practical, hands-on materials, Corwin continues to carry out the promise of its motto: **"Helping Educators Do Their Work Better."**